More Praise

"Great teams pursue innovation, and this book tells you how. Drawing on years of research, the authors offer a process you can use with your team. They show you what successful breakthrough teams do; they pull you toward your team's possibilities."

—**Geoff Bellman, consultant and author of** *Extraordinary Groups* **and** *Getting Things Done When You're Not in Charge*

"If you're looking to up your performance as a team or simply increase your chances of getting change adopted, you'll get there with *The Innovative Team*. Backed by research-based tools and twenty years of experience, this book teaches individuals and teams how increasing their awareness of the breakthrough thinking process can accelerate performance. From fable to process deep-dive, this is a must for your toolbox."

—**David Gonzalez, design and delivery manager, Center for Creative Leadership**

the innovative team

the innovative team

unleashing creative potential for breakthrough results

Chris Grivas
Gerard J. Puccio

JOSSEY-BASS
A Wiley Imprint
www.josseybass.com

Published by Jossey-Bass
A Wiley Imprint
One Montgomery Street, Suite 1200, San Francisco, CA 94104-4594—www.josseybass.com

Jossey-Bass books and products are available through most bookstores. To contact Jossey-Bass directly call our Customer Care Department within the U.S. at 800-956-7739, outside the U.S. at 317-572-3986, or fax 317-572-4002.

Wiley also publishes its books in a variety of electronic formats and by print-on-demand. Not all content that is available in standard print versions of this book may appear or be packaged in all book formats. If you have purchased a version of this book that did not include media that is referenced by or accompanies a standard print version, you may request this media by visiting http://booksupport.wiley.com. For more information about Wiley products, visit us at www.wiley.com.

Library of Congress Cataloging-in-Publication Data

Grivas, Chris, 1965–
    The innovative team : unleashing creative potential for breakthrough results / Chris Grivas and Gerard J. Puccio. – 1st ed.
        p. cm.
    Includes bibliographical references.
    ISBN 978-1-118-11571-8 (hardcoer); ISBN 978-1-118-15082-5 (ebk);
    ISBN 978-1-118-15083-2 (ebk.); ISBN 978-1-118-15084-9 (ebk.)
    1. Problem solving.   2. Creative thinking.   3. Creative ability in business.   4. Teams in the workplace–Management.   I. Puccio. Gerard J.   II. Title.
    HD30.29.G747 2012
    658.4'022–dc23   2011029331

Printed in the United States of America

FIRST EDITION

HB Printing   10 9 8 7 6 5 4 3 2 1

Contents

Acknowledgments

About fifteen years ago Gerard Puccio shared his initial FourSight theory and measure with Blair Miller and Sarah Thurber, who soon after became partners in establishing FourSight as a commercial venture. We wish to express our deepest gratitude to these FourSight partners whose painstaking efforts and commitment transformed FourSight into a visible, viable, and valuable concept and tool that has benefited people around the world. It was Blair who first recognized the potential to bring FourSight to a much larger audience and it was this vision that has enabled tens of thousands to benefit from the insights associated with the theory and measure. It was his ability to dream big while focusing on the pragmatic details that provided the right platform for FourSight to take off. And much appreciation is owed to Sarah Thurber, whose twin skills in the visual and written medium lifted the aesthetic quality of FourSight and the suite of FourSight products to a world-class level. Her ability to be part artist and part business manager is rare and invaluable in advancing FourSight and *The Innovative Team*.

As with most creative endeavors, this book took a team to make it happen. The authors are blessed to have a uniquely talented creative community of colleagues and friends to rely on when they needed support. In addition to Blair and Sarah, our "innovative team" also includes Jonathan Vehar, who was unfailingly generous with his own time and expertise, providing feedback and encouragement throughout the writing process. And perhaps most significantly, Erica Browne Grivas, whose imagination, humor, and deep commitment provided the breath for helping this book find life. She is by far the best writer in the family.

Several other colleagues and friends provided help, encouragement, and support (both moral and tactical) along the way. The authors are deeply grateful to Geoff Bellman, Rigby Biddle, Byron Schneider, Russ Schoen, JD Schramm, Nate Schwagler, and Susan Williams for their contributions to making this book a reality.

Thank you all!

About the Authors

Chris Grivas is an organizational development consultant who for more than fifteen years has been actively managing change and facilitating growth for leaders and companies worldwide, including Ernst & Young, Connecticut Children's Medical Center, New York University, and Blessing White. Whether consulting with individuals, teams, or entire organizations, Chris partners with his clients to customize comprehensive development approaches to support their unique needs and cultures. He helps teams come together, solve problems, and position themselves for future success. He consults with leaders on how they can develop themselves and build an organization designed to produce the behaviors and results they desire.

Exploring the nature of innovation and the corporate culture of creativity has long fascinated Chris since he earned his MS in creativity and innovation from the International Center for Studies in Creativity. Chris is qualified to use many psychological instruments, such as the Myers-Briggs Type Indicator, DiSC Behavior Styles Indicator, and a host of

360-degree and multi-rater instruments. One measure that he is particularly impressed by because of its ease of application and its focus on innovation is the FourSight measure, introduced by coauthor Gerard J. Puccio, which forms the basis for *The Innovative Team*.

Chris and Gerard first partnered on research examining the relationship between personality traits and creativity (published by *Creativity and Innovation Management*) and now have worked together on the book in your hand.

■ ■ ■

Gerard J. Puccio is the department chair and a professor at the International Center for Studies in Creativity, Buffalo State, a unique academic department that offers the world's only MS degree in creativity. In addition to creating the FourSight measure, Gerard has written more than fifty articles, chapters, and books. Along with his colleagues Marie Mance and Mary Murdock, he recently completed the second edition of a book titled *Creative Leadership: Skills That Drive Change* (2011). In recognition of his outstanding work as a scholar, Gerard received the State University of New York Chancellor's Recognition Award for Research Excellence and the President's Medal for Scholarship and Creativity.

Gerard is an accomplished speaker, trainer, and consultant; he has worked with major corporations, universities, and numerous school districts in the United States and around the world. Some of the organizations Gerard has worked with recently include the British Broadcasting Corporation (BBC), Paribas, Fisher-Price Brands, Rich Products, and Siemens. Gerard holds a PhD in organizational psychology from the University of Manchester, England.

Foreword

People have used their imaginations since the dawn of humanity to creatively resolve problems, to innovate, and to advance society. Unfortunately, for most of human history we have taken our creative thinking for granted, generally assuming that only a small number of gifted people were endowed with the ability to imagine and manifest new possibilities. Our own experiences, and now the scientific study of creativity, underscore the fact that we all engage in creative thinking – it's just something that all humans do. To varying degrees we all imagine and create our world. From your aunt who has always been clever with crafts to Nobel scientists who are recognized for their breakthrough thinking, we have all been endowed with minds that create. The question is, to what degree do you take advantage of this natural gift?

Although humans have always been creative, it was not until the middle of the twentieth century that psychologists began to closely examine, and scientifically study, this quality that fundamentally separates us from all other species on our planet. With more than six decades of research and thinking, numerous books and scholarly journals are now filled with information about the nature of creativity. Among many insights, one undeniable fact has emerged – creative thinking is a teachable and trainable skill.

It was my early work as a creativity trainer that led to the theory upon which this book is based. In the late 1980s I was working as part of a consulting team responsible for delivering creativity training to managers employed by Procter & Gamble. Our job was to train course participants in Creative Problem Solving, a well-established process and set of thinking tools, which could be used by these managers to more skillfully and deliberately apply their imaginations to business challenges and opportunities. It was over a coffee break during one of these corporate training programs that the seed of an idea was planted, an idea that over time grew, and is revealed in this book in the form of a fable.

Our training program was built upon a process proven to promote breakthrough thinking for problems that do not have easy answers. In broad terms, we taught participants how to look at challenges and opportunities from new perspectives, how to use their imaginations to generate original ideas, ways to evaluate and strengthen the most promising solutions, and how to navigate resistance to new propositions so that their breakthroughs might be more readily adopted. The training program featured principles, tools, and strategies that reinforced success in each of these areas of the creative process. After facilitating participants through a creative decision-making tool used to systematically evaluate and refine the most promising solutions, two managers engaged me in a conversation over coffee. The first manager, let's use the name Pat, quickly approached me to relay how difficult it was for her to learn this tool. Pat felt a good deal of frustration in having to be so deliberate, specific, and objective in rating each one of her options against a formal set of criteria. It wasn't just what Pat said but how she said it that had an impact on me. Her tone and body language clearly highlighted that the use of this tool was a real struggle for her.

Feeling bad about subjecting someone to an apparently painful learning experience, I continued with my coffee break. Only a few more minutes into this break, another manager approached me. Let's call him Fred. Fred put his hand on my shoulder and with a smile on his face expressed deep gratitude for teaching him the same decision-making tool that Pat had found so difficult. Fred explained that the tool fit perfectly with his natural approach to making choices and that he now had a structured method for being even more deliberate and systematic in evaluating and developing competing options. It was a good thing for me that the conversation with Fred closely followed my chat with Pat, as it lifted my spirits before reengaging the group in the training course.

These opposing reactions served as a catalyst for what grew into a theory and measure called FourSight. The coffee break conversations made me realize that people had their own naturally built-in way of engaging in creative thinking. That is to say, I realized that while creative thinking is natural to all humans, not all humans engage in creative thinking in the same way. Psychologists refer to this as cognitive style, which means that people will differ in terms of how they prefer to organize and process information. The FourSight theory and measure helps people to identify their preferences within the creative process. In hindsight, it is now clear to me that Pat and Fred simply had different creative-thinking preferences.

Working with colleagues, most notably Blair Miller and Sarah Thurber, over the last twenty years or so, we have discovered that most people report having higher levels of energy for some areas of the creative process over others. We refer to these four creative-thinking preference types as Clarifiers, Ideators, Developers, and Implementers. Each way of thinking is fundamental to the creative process; that is, you need all four to generate breakthroughs, but our research and applied work has highlighted the fact that people will vary in regard to how comfortable they are thinking and behaving as Clarifiers, Ideators, Developers, and Implementers. Granted, there are those individuals who show an equal level of energy across all four preferences; we refer to these folks as Integrators as they are equally comfortable drawing on any one of these four breakthrough-thinking preferences. Looking back at the coffee-break conversations, my hypothesis now is that Pat was probably an Ideator and therefore was challenged by the decision-making tool, while

Fred was most likely a Developer who has a good deal of energy for evaluative thinking.

Over this time period we have conducted more than a dozen research studies that have helped us to understand further the personalities, skills, attitudes, and preferences of Clarifiers, Ideators, Developers, Implementers, and Integrators. At the same time we have had tens of thousands of individuals from around the world use the FourSight measure as part of their professional development. This applied work has reinforced and extended two key areas of value associated with FourSight: benefits for individuals and teams.

First, the value of knowing FourSight preferences at an individual level include:

- recognizing your strengths and natural areas of comfort as you engage in the thinking required to come up with breakthroughs

- understanding your blind spots, and potential areas of pitfalls, as you move through the creative process

- learning what areas of thinking you need to develop to become a more creative powerhouse

Second, with respect to teams and working with others in general, the benefits of knowing your own and others' FourSight preferences include:

- transitioning from the use of judgmental or negative labels, especially when someone has a different way of thinking from you, to an appreciation of differences, thus creating a more positive climate for creative thinking

- reducing tension or conflict on a team that has diverse FourSight preferences by helping members recognize how these differences may lead to frustration, sometimes hidden and sometimes overt, when working together to solve problems or produce breakthrough ideas

- improving overall performance by revealing biases a team might possess with respect to the creative process which allows the team to be certain that they are adequately addressing all areas of the creative process

This book is focused primarily on the benefits of FourSight for a team. It reveals how awareness of FourSight preferences, one's own and others', can help a team improve performance by appreciating and leveraging diverse thinking preferences. Additionally, it shows how the formal application of the steps of the creative process represented by the four FourSight preferences, i.e., clarifying the problem, generating ideas, developing solutions, and implementing action, enables a team to produce innovative breakthroughs.

This book was written to help teams take advantage of the creative talents of their team members to help teams sustain their innovation efforts by recognizing that innovation does not have to be left up to chance. Instead, a formal process can be used to produce breakthrough thinking, and to recognize that within this process people will have different preferences.

The ideas contained in this book are based on years of research and application. FourSight has been around for twenty years and the Creative Problem Solving process has been used in a variety of settings and studied by various researchers for over fifty years. Given this body of work, I am confident that the content of this book will prove beneficial to you and your team's innovation efforts.

Gerard J. Puccio, PhD
Buffalo, NY

the innovative team

Introduction

We live in an era of accelerated change unlike any other in history. Products become obsolete faster than ever before, new careers suddenly appear while others quickly vanish, organizations rise and fall almost overnight, and just trying to keep up with technology can make your head spin. All of this means we face more and more situations that require creative responses as the old ways of doing things falter and fade. Be honest. How well prepared are you to employ new thinking to seize the opportunities and resolve the challenges brought by change? If you believe there is room for you to be more effective at managing change you are in good company—even some of the most successful executives feel unnerved by today's unrelenting waves of adjustment. An IBM study of more than fifteen hundred executives around the world showed that an overwhelming majority of seasoned leaders were not fully confident that they were prepared to respond effectively to rapid change.[1] Their number one suggestion? Adopt creativity as a core leadership skill. As Lee Iacocca, former CEO of Chrysler observed, "Leadership is all about managing change—whether you are leading a company or a country. Things change, and you get creative."[2]

The faster things change, many experts say, the stronger your creative thinking and problem-solving skills need to be. To successfully compete in the twenty-first century, leaders are calling for increased training in creative problem solving everywhere from boardrooms to elementary classrooms.

This is why so many organizations emphasize innovation—new products, new services, new business models, new markets, new forms of operations, and so on. Look at your own organization's vision, mission, or values statement. If it is like most, innovation will be mentioned prominently. Everyone strives to be innovative but few succeed. Why? *The reality is that organizations have a hard time being truly innovative without awareness of how they use their creative resources.*

If creativity and innovation are important to the success of your organization, how skillful are you in making the most of your teams' natural creative talents?

First let's look at how you solve problems. If you were to describe how you recently improved something, resolved a problem, or came up with a breakthrough to a perplexing challenge, your process would probably look a lot like this: you begin your efforts by gathering some information about the task at hand. At the very least, you might do an Internet search to look at the history, gather data, or seek out others' experiences with similar situations. Once you feel you have enough information, you start coming up with ideas. You will probably continue to look for potential options until you hit on one that you think will do the trick. From there you take the idea and tinker with it, trying to make sure it will work before putting it into action. Finally, you make the change and watch for the desired results. When it works, you are filled with satisfaction. When it doesn't, you revisit this process to see where things went wrong and take corrective action. Did you miss a key piece of information? Were there better approaches for addressing the situation? Was your solution fully worked out? Did you take a misstep while implementing the solution?

This creative thought process allows humans to imagine new possibilities and then to bring these breakthroughs to life. It has been around throughout human history—since we first needed to hunt for our food—but scientists only began researching it over the last fifty years or so, and until then we never really understood how the creative process worked. What does the research tell us?

- *The creative process is universal.* All humans with normally functioning brains engage in creative thinking. We apply our creative thinking to everyday problems, such as when you are missing an ingredient to a recipe or a part to a broken piece of machinery, and to larger societal problems, such as keeping the economy moving forward, reducing crime, or improving education.

- *The creative process has four predictable steps to it.* A central theme of this book is that the creative process can be boiled down to four distinct steps: clarify the situation, generate ideas, develop solutions, and implement plans. Whether you are a CEO, a plumber, an artisanal cheese maker, or someone planning a birthday party, you follow this pattern when you need to use your imagination to improve the way things are done, develop new products, or fix things that are broken.

- *We are not all equally creative, but we can improve our creativity.* Sorry to say that we are not all Edisons, Fords, Zuckerbergs, Rowlings, Spielbergs, or Angelous. The good news is no matter what your natural set point is for creative thinking, it can be enhanced through training and practice. More than seventy research studies agree that individuals can be taught to be more effective creative thinkers.[3]

More than just a professional skill, creative thinking is also a life skill. You face challenges and opportunities in your personal life that require you to think in new ways. Consider the opportunities and challenges that come along with relationships, with parenting, with managing a household, with pursing your biggest dreams. Life comes with challenges but these challenges are much, much easier when we face them with creative thinking.

That is what this book is about—the most important thing we all do every day—think. Specifically, *The Innovative Team* is about focused creative thinking that allows us to successfully respond to situations that do not have easy answers or immediately apparent solutions. It is an understandable source of practical knowledge about the natural process we all use when solving real-world problems. It is designed to demystify the topics of creativity and innovation so that they are accessible to everyone. The authors have worked with thousands of individuals and hundreds of teams worldwide to successfully direct their creativity toward solving complex challenges. Gerard Puccio has served as the department chair of the International Center for Studies in Creativity at Buffalo State (State University of New York) since 1997 and is the creator of the FourSight theory and measure, which assess individual and team preferences within the creative process and provide the core concepts explored in this book. Chris Grivas has been an organizational development consultant since 1996, enhancing leadership and innovation skills and processes in an array of industries for academic, health care, nonprofit, and financial services entities, strengthening leadership and teamwork skills at every level of the organization.

Thinking Differently

According to researchers and scientists, our high level of cognition (and strategically placed thumbs) is what sets us apart from the much of the natural world. But although we all think, it turns out that we do not all think in the same way.

Research shows us that although we all follow the four steps of the creative thought process, we exhibit different thinking preferences within the process. The revelation here is that people will choose to spend more time in one area over another. Some people, by nature, like to spend time analyzing and clarifying the situation, others are more blue sky or big picture thinkers who continually generate big ideas, some will tirelessly focus on developing and perfecting the solution, and yet others are much more concerned with implementing the plan and moving to the next project. Think of this as a kind of diversity—one not determined by someone's demographic background but a diversity of the mind. In fact, two people with the same background, even siblings raised together, may approach problems in very different ways. When such differences exist, especially on working teams (and they almost always do), there is potential for misunderstanding, frustration, judgment, and conflict.

Understanding how we think and our preferences for approaching challenges can help us work and live our lives with a higher degree of satisfaction and success. To this end, psychologists have been working on tools, called *measures*, for understanding our behavior, and although no one measure can reflect the full complexity of human nature, the best of these measures can help us make sense of parts of ourselves and how we interact with the world.

Some measures, such as the Myers-Briggs Type Indicator (MBTI), help sort out personalities—our own and of those around us. Are we introverted or extraverted? Do we make decisions based on facts or on our gut instincts? Others, such as the DiSC Behavior Styles Indicator, help us become more aware of our behaviors. When we try to get things done, are we first concerned with tasks or people? Are we focused on potentials or realities? Given your preferences, you can understand why you and your coworker might butt heads or why after a party your friend is always tired while you are ready for more (or vice versa).

A New Framework

Such frameworks are enormously helpful in the workplace, helping us do everything from developing teamwork strategies to honing individual career paths. Through a combination of storytelling and practical tips, this book introduces a framework called FourSight. Tempered by more than a decade of real-world field testing in corporate and nonprofit settings on six continents, FourSight is built on over twenty years of solid scientific research that examines human creativity and invention. FourSight helps answer the fundamental question, "Where do I prefer to spend my energy within the creative process?"

FourSight enables teams to understand their patterns of thinking and then to more deliberately manage themselves to accomplish a task. What sets FourSight apart from other frameworks is that it goes beyond personality to hone in on what happens when your individual personality is confronted with the task of solving problems creatively. The more you know about the way you think, the more you can deliberately use your strengths. If you need to get to some breakthrough thinking, looking at your (and your team's) preferences for the creative process will enable you to alter your usual patterns, use your time more effectively, and generate new productivity.

What's Ahead

To introduce you to the model of creative thinking and to help you see how different thinking preferences might play out in a team working together, we begin with a story of a team that has not been functioning well, has produced lackluster results, and needs to come up with something good before getting canned by the client. It's a story designed to get you thinking about yourself in the creative process and how your natural tendencies have influenced your experiences in working on teams charged with generating innovative solutions. What are your preferences (clarifying, generating, developing, implementing)? How might your preferences affect others? By understanding your place in the creative process, you will generate better outcomes and higher satisfaction in your work and personal life.

As a leader, you have to lead people who think differently from you as well as those who may have similar preferences. Each present challenges; Part Two of this book helps you identify specific strategies that you can use to more effectively lead others. As a team member, this section will also help you better understand your role in the team and why the team may be working the way that it does. The second half of the book is designed to give you a brief description of the FourSight framework and help you explore ways to make it applicable in your day-to-day work within teams. As a result, you'll come to know and appreciate that not all people use their creativity the same way and that no one way or combination of ways is perfect for every situation. It's the understanding of yourself and others on your team that will create the conditions for successful innovation to grow.

Just one reminder before diving in—we are all naturally creative. Therefore, the question is not *whether* you are creative, because you are. To boost your creativity, the more helpful approach is to understand exactly in what *way* you are creative and then to explicitly leverage and build your creative-thinking powers. The more we understand ourselves and how we think, the more we can consciously apply ourselves effectively. Once that happens, there's no limit to the innovative breakthrough results you and your team can achieve.

Notes

1. IBM. (2010). *Capitalising on complexity: Insights from the global chief executive officer (CEO) study.* Portsmouth: UK: Author.

2. Iacocca, L. (2007). *Where have all the leaders gone?* New York: Scribner.

3. Scott, G. M., Leritz, L. E., & Mumford, M. D. (2004). The effectiveness of creativity training: A meta-analysis. *Creativity Research Journal, 16,* 361–388.

part 1

The Story

chapter 1

We Have a Problem

"There is *no way* this is going to work."

Juan Alvarez's statement hung in the air like an oversized anvil ready to crush his two team members sitting across the conference table. "Why would Tony give this account to a new leader with virtually no exposure to the client?"

Elaine Cassidy chimed in, "Look, Juan, you've seen the status report. We've been working the Consolidated account for a year and they've rejected most of what we've given them. Maybe it's a good idea to bring in a fresh set of eyes."

"Of course, their dissatisfaction is my big concern as well," retorted Juan. "I guess I am just surprised that when they moved Jane out they wouldn't look within this team for a new leader. After all, we know the client very well."

"I am glad they didn't look within," added Damon from the other end of the conference table. "I'd hate to have to report to you, Juan." The three of them laughed nervously because they knew Damon wasn't exactly joking. Quickly, he changed the subject. "What do you suppose Consolidated is looking for? I thought our report had some great ideas."

"All I heard from Tony is that they weren't very happy. But I thought we gave them what they wanted and right on time—the way we always have. I have no idea what they could have been looking for that we didn't provide," said Elaine.

"I know what made them dissatisfied," Juan said quietly, staring at the conference table. He knew he was about to cause a stir but he was frustrated with his two teammates and something needed to change. He saw their approaches as the problem and now felt as if he were being held accountable for their mistakes. He thought their behavior had cost him the job of taking over as team leader.

"We didn't spend enough time finding a new direction," he said. He spoke softly at first but his voice began to rise. "You guys wouldn't let me finish the data analysis. I was closing in on something new that Consolidated hadn't explored but I just couldn't go far enough." He motioned to Damon. "Not with you always jumping in with new solutions and pulling us in new directions." He turned to Elaine. "And you pressuring us to get the reports out the door."

"Hey, that's not fair." Elaine felt her shoulders tense and her face flush. "If I didn't keep you guys on task, we'd never have gotten anything done."

"Being on task is one thing. Rushing a poor product out the door is another," Juan responded, unwilling to conceal his frustration. "My guess is the client could see that our recommendations weren't really thought through. We could have done that if you had given me more time to finish analyzing the data. Plus, you could have helped instead of leaving all the analysis to me."

"Hey, Juan, that's enough. We're all in this together," Damon cut in. "Elaine and I did try to help with the analysis. You just didn't seem to know when enough was enough. Eventually, we had to move past the data and start thinking up some solutions for the client's problems." Damon didn't want to rile up Juan any more but he still felt the need to defend himself. "That was my contribution. When problems emerged from the data, I would come up with ideas. If I hadn't been exploring different possible solutions, you'd still be wallowing in that data."

"Yeah, you'd present solutions all right—so many it's a miracle we were able to consolidate the report into manageable chunks," Juan answered. "We don't always need to explore every possible option, Damon. A few workable ideas would be plenty . . ."

Just then, new team members Maya Russo and Amy Satori entered the room and the sparring came to an abrupt halt. Juan, Damon, and Elaine regained their composure and introduced themselves. Seconds later, Tony Martin, the senior partner in charge of the engagement, appeared at the conference room door. He cut a handsome figure with his tanned complexion, graying temples, and designer suit. Turning with a charismatic smile, he ushered in Kate Murdock, their new team leader. Following some chilly greetings, Tony took his seat at the end of the conference table. Kate went to the windows and opened the blinds, allowing the midday sun to enter the room. Then she settled in next to Tony. Although she matched his professional demeanor, Kate added her own warmth and approachability. Fit and focused, nothing seemed to escape her blue eyes as she quietly surveyed the team.

Tony began: "I can't stay for the whole meeting, so let's get right down to business," he said. "As you know, Consolidated has been less than pleased by our efforts to date. Our contact actually said that what we've given her so far is nothing that another firm couldn't have given her for half the price. I don't think I need to emphasize that Consolidated is one of our premier clients. We built our name on innovation, and with client feedback like this, we are putting that reputation—and our futures—at risk."

Members of the original team—Damon, Elaine, and Juan—looked as if they had just been steamrolled. Maya and

Amy seemed outwardly calmer but no one really understood what had gone wrong.

They had done everything that was asked of them—why wasn't that enough? Maya and Amy were silently questioning the competence of the others and wondering what they'd gotten themselves into by joining this project. Tony recognized their deer-in-the-headlights expressions. Good, he thought with satisfaction, but I've got to drive this point home.

After a pause, he forged on. "A reputation for being innovative is what separates us from our competition. It helps us maintain a special place in the market, and we cannot afford to compromise it. That is why I've decided to make some changes within this team. You all are aware that Jane has been reassigned to a new client engagement. To take over her role, I have recruited Kate Murdock here as your new team leader. Although she's never worked on the Consolidated account, she's had some experience turning this type of situation around. I think you're going to like her approach. I've also asked Amy and Maya here to join this assignment because they both bring some specialized expertise."

"Amy brings a strong background in data integration, so now you have a technology expert." Amy smiled, unconvincingly, somewhat embarrassed at being introduced as an "expert."

"And Maya, although fairly new to the firm, has a background in consulting to manufacturing firms like Consolidated. I'm sure she'll bring some fresh thinking to the group."

Maya managed a stiff nod.

"That said, I'd like to introduce you to Kate Murdock. Kate, everyone." A riff of awkward nods and nervous smiles bounced around the table toward Kate. "Kate has a grounding in the concepts and processes around innovation. Her last team created some eye-opening opportunities for a client. That sounds like just the medicine for Consolidated. Kate?"

"Thanks, Tony," Kate began. She sat forward and looked at the group. "That's some pretty harsh criticism from Consolidated. I imagine those of you who have worked on this account are wondering exactly what happened. I'm sure you worked hard to give Consolidated what they asked for. Clearly that wasn't enough. I can understand that you are disappointed but today we're starting fresh."

The tension around the table was thick. Kate wished Tony had not been so blunt with his feedback. She was threatening enough as the newcomer. Now she had to earn the team's trust and respect while they felt attacked. It wouldn't be easy. The best thing to do is to get them talking, she thought.

"Before we get started with setting our new direction, I think it's important we get to know each other a little bit," Kate asserted with a little too much urgency in her voice. "Let's go around the table. Tell me not just your name and roles but also one thing you really like doing when it comes to being part of a team charged with solving a problem. What's something you enjoy focusing on?"

No one on the team was prepared for this question. Her gaze met with blank stares all around the table. Several people wondered if Kate was playing some kind of game. They weren't sticking their necks out for that!

Kate decided to lead by example.

"I'll start. I'm Kate Murdock. As Tony mentioned, for the last year I have been leading the innovation efforts in our corporate manufacturing division. Although I haven't been working on the Consolidated account, I have been leading client-centered teams, like this one, on client engagement in the manufacturing sector. I would say the part of the process I enjoy most is coming up with ideas and making sure they fit the client's needs. I like to sort through ideas, develop some into great solutions, and put them into action."

Damon was the first to play along. Damon was a tall, handsome African American man in whom everything seemed to be built on a grand scale—whether it was his full-tilt good spirits, broad shoulders, or his infectious smile. Damon instantly struck Kate as the guy who would know everybody at a party and whom everyone would want to know.

"OK. I'll go first. I'm Damon Miller. I'm the marketing analyst on the team and I guess what I enjoy most is . . . finding the recommendations for the client. I thought we had some good ideas for Consolidated, so I can't tell you how disappointed I am with this reaction."

"Thanks, Damon," said Kate. "Yes, this reaction stings, I know. But I'm told you guys are one of the hardest working teams of managers we have. I'm confident we'll turn Consolidated around. So you like coming up with ideas then, Damon?"

"Oh, boy, does he," chimed in Elaine, to the delight of the team as well as Kate—for quite different reasons. "Once he gets going, you can't shut him down!"

"It's kind of my thing," admitted Damon.

"Hi, Kate," Elaine jumped in. "I'm Elaine Cassidy and I'm a business analyst. One of several here." Elaine was perhaps the eldest of the group. She was a large woman in her late fifties who, judging by the paleness of her skin, didn't get outside much. She projected the impatient air of having been there, done that. She seemed to want to get right down to business.

"Nice to meet you, Elaine. What is the thing you like to focus on most?" said Kate, thinking that Elaine was a what-you-see-is-what-you-get type of person.

"I like to get the product to the client. I like to make sure we have a strong deliverable and that our recommendations are ready to go."

"So that sounds like you like to refine and develop the work and put it into action, is that right?"

"Yes and no. Refining and developing is what I need other team members for. I like to put the plan into action. I like to get it done."

"And quick!" added Juan, smiling at Elaine.

"Too quick, Juan?" asked Kate knowingly.

"Well, Elaine knows that sometimes I feel she might rush us along a bit."

"Yes," agreed Elaine reluctantly. "We've talked about that. But I do make sure we get results!"

"Yes, you do," Juan conceded.

"Nice," said Kate, making some notes. "Who's next?"

"I'll go, I guess," said Amy Satori, looking understated in a plain tan sweater and matching tan slacks. Amy had an air of quiet confidence. She was lean and poised, probably in her late thirties, with jet black hair and designer glasses. She sat with her chin resting on her hands as if she were continually contemplating the underlying meaning of the conversation at hand. "I'm Amy Satori, the data integration specialist, and I guess that's where I like to spend my time. I like going deep into data and getting a real clear picture of a situation. If I don't have a clear picture of what's happening, it's kind of hard to move forward with confidence. I keep thinking we've missed something. I guess, in the case with Consolidated, something must have been missed. Either that or we just didn't put enough time into developing our ideas into solutions that really worked."

"Thank you, Amy. Let's not worry about that now. I'm sure we all are trying to sort out what happened here—and that's normal—but let's focus on moving forward. I'm confident we are going to 'wow' this client. So, Amy, it sounds like you like to spend your time clarifying the issues, gathering the facts. Is that right?"

"Yes, but that's not all. I also like to come up with solutions and work with them to make them strong, to turn good concepts into great solutions. I like to take the time to weigh different solutions and then turn the best into something great. When I get done, I'll have something that I know will work. It drove Elaine a bit crazy on the last project we worked on together," Amy added sheepishly. "I like to be thorough and she's ready to move things into action. But I'm glad Elaine is here because she has so much energy for that last push." Amy was pleased that Kate seemed so interested in her right off the bat. Kate nodded her head and made a few more notes.

"I'll go next," said Maya, the youngest member of the team. In her mid-twenties, she looked every bit the professional on the rise. She was tanned, wore stylish glasses, large hoop earrings, and bobbed brown hair perfectly coiffed. She spoke with a hint of a New York accent. "I am Maya Russo and I'm an associate business analyst. I guess I don't really know where I have the most fun spending my time. I've been active in each part of the engagement process in the past couple of years. As people are describing what they like to do, I'm listening and thinking, 'yeah, I like to do that, too.' I guess you'll see how that plays out as we work together."

"Thanks, Maya. That's fine. It sounds like you can relate to everyone's strengths, which is a strength in and of itself. I appreciate your sharing that. OK, I guess you're next." Kate motioned toward Juan.

Juan was a Hispanic man in his forties with an Ivy League education and the easy confidence that goes with it. Wearing a tie and jacket, a cut above the business-casual culture of the firm, he carried a sense of authority. He was large, stuffy, and clearly not happy with his team. He shifted in his seat.

"I'm Juan Alvarez, senior business analyst. I guess I'm like Amy in that I like to get into the data and work on making the solutions we come up with stronger. If I don't get enough time to really sort through the information, I just won't be happy with the end result. I need to be able to get my arms around something, whether it's the problem itself or our recommended solution. I need the time to get to know it well."

"Thank you, Juan. I like the way you described that—'get your arms around it.' I know what you mean," said Kate. "OK. Now, Tony, how about you?"

Tony leaned back and smiled. "I like it when engagements go well and we have happy clients! It's my job to manage that relationship so that we produce something of value for our clients. I get to know them and I get to know what makes them tick. I guess I like to gather data, like some of you, but I also like seeing something happen with that data. I'm not above having fun, either. Sometimes, I think that helps us relax and look at things a little differently." Tony could tell that last statement surprised some of the team members because he saw eyes grow wide and eyebrows go up around the table. He smiled again, adding, "I hope you'll get to see that as we move forward. But it should be no surprise that I also am focused on the bottom line. When our clients are happy, I'm happy."

"Thanks, Tony," followed Kate. "The way you've all described yourselves helps me quite a bit. Not only do I see where we're strong as a team but I also have an idea of how I might be helpful to you and how I might leverage your support. I need help where some of you have said you are strong. As an example: I don't have a lot of patience when it comes to gathering information. I get what I need and then go. I've learned that I need to slow down and make sure I have all the information before I move forward. It's not easy for me but I solve problems more effectively when I do it. So I'm committed to gathering all the facts we need. I have a feeling Juan and Amy are going to hold me to that."

Juan and Amy looked at each other and made a nonverbal pact to do just that. The team members looked quizzically at Kate, intrigued that their new team leader would reveal a flaw so early in their relationship. Internally, each member spun this differently. Juan thought it might be a sign of weakness. Elaine wondered what the point was. Amy and Damon thought it set a nice tone, and Maya could relate to Kate's admission right away.

"Well," Tony interposed, "I'd say it looks like you all are on your way to getting to know each other and have a fresh start with Consolidated. I'm going to take my leave, but Kate and I have agreed to weekly updates, so I'll be hearing how things are going. Part of my job is serving the client directly. To do that, I have to make sure you have what you need. That includes both resources and time directly with the client, should you find that helpful. Just please let me know how I can help as things move forward."

He stood to go. "Good seeing everyone. Oh, just one more thought before I leave. Listening to the feedback from Consolidated may have been rough but it's essential. This client is flat-out asking for a new direction. That's what I expect: new directions. You are on this team because I think you're the right people for this challenge. Take care, now."

"See you at lunch, Kate," he added as he gently closed the conference room door behind him.

Kate thought she sensed the tension relax—if only for a moment. But she knew things were about to get much more tense before they got better.

chapter 2

Just What Kind of Duck Are We Dealing with Here?

A lone with her new team for the first time, Kate got right down to business. Clearly, the team was disconcerted by the client's feedback. She sensed that the team was drowning, mired in feelings of failure and confusion. Rather than skirt the issue, she dove right in. Avoidance was not an option. This team needed to move on. Fast.

Kate broke the silence. "So what do you understand to be the source of Consolidated's dissatisfaction?"

Damon spoke first. "That's a bit of a mystery," he said. "Not to sound too defensive, but we produced and presented two key reports. We covered the marketplace thoroughly and I think we had solid recommendations."

"I know we did," Juan added. "I went through the data for weeks. We didn't miss a thing. And Alicia was there for both presentations."

"Wait, sorry. Who is Alicia?" asked Maya.

"She's a senior VP at Consolidated," said Kate. "She's our main contact there. She's the one who said we didn't deliver anything that another firm couldn't have delivered for half the price. What do you think she means?"

Juan was immediately defensive. "I have no idea. Our client engagement contract offers very clear guidelines as to what to expect from us as a firm. It's like she expected divine intervention."

"Maybe not divine," piped up Elaine, "but clearly Alicia was looking for more than the standard market analysis, projections, and recommendations we did provide." Elaine sat with her arms folded across her chest, looking impatient with all this hypothesizing. "Kate, have you spoken with Alicia? Do you know anything we haven't heard?"

"Actually, I am going to talk with her in an hour. What questions should I ask?"

"How about 'Where did we go wrong?'" said Juan, frustrated. "I've never heard of a client calling for more innovation from our firm. That's what we're known for."

"Juan, come on," Elaine interjected. "Let's just ask her to be crystal clear about her expectations. What would make this a winning engagement?"

"What additional data would she like to see?" Amy chimed in. "You know, where else should we be looking?"

"I'll ask," answered Kate, "but honestly, she might be looking to us for that. What else?"

"Did you read the report?" asked Amy. "No offense to those of you here who worked on it, but it was pretty standard stuff for our industry. Don't get me wrong, it was well reasoned and seemed thorough. I just wouldn't call it 'innovative.'"

"I'm wondering what kinds of ideas she wants," said Damon. "It's true. What we gave her was pretty safe. We didn't exactly stretch the boundaries. Sounds like she wants something a little more novel."

"Novel, maybe. But *how* novel?" Juan responded. "Too much novelty and she'll think we're nuts."

"OK. So I need to gauge her openness to new ideas then?" Kate interjected, noticing Juan's resistance to Damon's push for new possibilities. Kate wondered if this dynamic had contributed to a lackluster product.

Juan pressed his point. "Most companies, especially established ones such as Consolidated, like to stick to their base . . . stay close to what made them successful. I'd be surprised if they are looking for something paradigm breaking."

Kate responded, "That is an assumption worth checking, Juan. I'll be sure to ask."

"An assumption?" Elaine echoed thoughtfully. "That's an interesting word. I wonder what other assumptions we've been operating under."

"Yes!" said Damon excitedly. "That may be just what's been getting in our way. What have we been assuming?"

"Frankly, the report you presented is what I assume our clients want," said Maya. "I'm pretty new here but all the client engagement teams I've worked with produced basically the same thing. Pretty cut-and-dried stuff."

Kate built on that. "The end product may have been cut and dried because you followed the standard way of doing things rather than look for a different angle."

Elaine was feeling defensive. "But we pulled data from all the most reliable sources. We presented a clear situational analysis and the ideas we recommended flowed logically from the data."

"Tell me about those ideas," Kate said.

"From my perspective, they made sense. Data point A led to point B. It flowed naturally," Elaine said.

"Funny thing about things that flow," said Kate, "they tend to go where there is least resistance. What about novelty? Did we include anything Alicia wouldn't have thought of herself? Was there anything there that might have altered the flow of reasoning?" asked Kate.

Elaine paused to consider. "No. I guess not. Like I said, the situation seemed pretty cut and dried, but maybe that was another assumption we made: we assumed we knew what was going on rather than exploring it further. I have to admit, I am probably guilty of that. I like to get things out the door. I don't always spend time questioning the situation. You know what I mean? If it's a duck, it's a duck. I don't care what kind of duck or what the duck is thinking about. It's a duck! Call it a duck and move on."

Kate smiled, "So you thought it was a duck. What if it's a swan?"

"Oooh, I like that," Damon said.

Elaine knew they were playing with her but wanted to keep things on track. "So you're saying that just because it has feathers, webbed feet, a beak, and floats on the water, it may not be what we think it is." She regretted this statement as soon as it left her lips. It would be hard to get back on track now.

"Maybe it is," said Kate. "Maybe you don't have enough information to know. What else could influence your decision? What color is it? What part of the world does it live in?"

"How much does it weigh? Where does it winter?" Amy played along.

"Does it quack or honk?" Damon chimed in, gleefully. "Could be a goose."

"And if it honks, what kind of honk is it? A goose or a swan?" Maya added her two cents.

"What if it didn't make much noise at all? Would it be a coot?" asked Juan, not wanting to be left out.

"No." Elaine had had enough of this ridiculousness. "That would be a dead duck."

chapter 3

The Sum of the Parts

Kate hung up the phone and sank back in her chair. She felt exhausted from her phone call with Alicia. It had already been a taxing morning and now she was late for lunch with Tony. In the elevator on the way up to the rooftop restaurant, Alicia's words rattled in Kate's head: "stale ... predictable ... nothing new," she had said. Clearly, the morning's discussion about novelty was on target. Consolidated was looking for a breakthrough, and judging by Alicia's skeptical tone, she wasn't too sure she was going to get it from Kate's team.

Tony had already ordered and was inspecting a plate of Alaskan salmon by the time she got to the table.

"I'm so sorry I'm late," she began. "I just got off the phone with Alicia."

"That's quite all right. I hope you don't mind that I didn't wait. I have another meeting at 1:30. Try the salmon," Tony said. "It's flown in fresh every day. Fabulous stuff."

"Sounds perfect. So, Tony, what did you think of the first meeting?"

"I'd say you are off to an interesting start. I like that you asked folks where they liked to spend their time while working for the client. It was a clever way to get into how they think. I think I got to know each of them more thanks to that."

"Thanks. Me, too. I can tell I've got a nice mixture of styles on the team. After you left, I learned even more."

"Tell me ..."

"I think those who are driven to implement haven't been giving their teammates time to clarify. When I asked why Consolidated isn't satisfied, I got the sense that pressure to get the product out the door had limited their creativity. They had sprinted to the finished product without exploring novel options that might be real opportunities for the client."

"What was driving that?"

"Actually, that was a question I had for you," said Kate. "What can you tell me about how this team's priorities were managed in the past year?"

"Jane was leading the team. She is very results focused. She's known as a real driver. It's a point of pride with her to deliver reports early. She met all her deadlines and frankly we were all impressed because her products were very much in line with those we produced for other clients. In retrospect, we may have been guilty of not paying enough attention. We woke up abruptly when Alicia threatened to take her business elsewhere."

"No doubt," replied Kate. "After talking with Alicia, I have a better understanding of her context. Consolidated is looking to expand. They are focusing on mergers and acquisitions and on product development. Frankly, I wonder why they aren't looking at process improvements, but that's for another time. Alicia believes they're in a great position to drive innovation in the market and put pressure on their competitors. That's not what they read in our recommendations. She found our take on Consolidated too conservative. She supported her position with data we hadn't even factored into our reports. It may be that our rush to completion squashed not only innovation but also shortchanged the research that influenced the team's perception of the market."

"So the team ended up recommending solutions to the wrong problem?"

"I'd even go further. I think the recommendations the team generated reflected their own assumptions about the market rather than reality," said Kate. "But I think they began to realize that this morning."

"Are they moving toward a solution?" asked Tony.

"It's too soon for a solution. They don't yet have a framework for understanding the process that led them off track."

"How do you expect these folks to think about process?" began Tony. "This firm has been in business for more than fifty years. We have consistently provided world-class research and results for our clients. We have our methods and this team knows them well. Are you ready to have the conversation that says the way they have been doing things all along has been misguided and they now need to look at doing things differently?"

"Gaining insights into yourself doesn't have to be painful or fly in the face of past experience," Kate insisted. "In fact, if the insights are honest, past experience will validate what you find. The past will become better understood."

"We aren't a firm known for self-reflection, Kate. You know that. We don't spend a lot of time thinking about our process. The guy who hired me wouldn't have had any patience for that kind of talk. We are about innovation. That's certain. Our focus is on results, not process."

"Yes. That works fine if you are not worried about occasionally missing the mark or wasting some effort. I would argue that because this firm is so well established, we haven't been too worried about that. This team, however, should be worried. We have a dissatisfied client, a big one. We have to think differently. Without developing an awareness of their process, this team is sure to produce the same misguided product they did the first time. I'm not going against the cultural norm at this firm. If this team wants innovation and results, they need self-awareness and process awareness to get them."

"You know, I agree with you. I just want to be sure you are prepared for potential pushback. People might see it as a waste of time and you need to get their buy-in to do something different. If they don't believe examining their process is useful, then it's not." Tony paused, took another bite of salmon, and asked, "What's your plan?"

"I'll start with the need. The team is already rattled by the feedback from Consolidated. That may be enough for them to try something new."

"And then?" Tony challenged.

"It's time to put some names on the behaviors I've seen so far. It's the only way they can become more aware of what they are doing. This morning, when I asked what they liked to do, did you notice how people answered? I think I can help them relate their own experience to terms in the breakthrough thinking process. I can help them get some language down about how they work together and the process they must follow to produce something valuable for our client. Once they have an understanding of the breakthrough thinking process, we can be more deliberate moving forward." Kate paused as she considered the personalities on her team. "There may be some tension that will prove useful."

"How so?"

"Well, Damon clearly loves to generate ideas. He's a divergent thinker. He loves the challenge of coming up with as many options as he can. Elaine is all about delivering the goods. I'm guessing that between Elaine and their old team leader, Jane, Damon felt pretty squeezed. With their drive to completion, I bet they found Damon's propensity to explore ideas inefficient. I have a hunch they rushed him along. Their emphasis was outcome, not novelty. Meanwhile, Juan would like to have spent more time sorting through the data and clarifying the situation before moving forward to Damon's ideas. I think the addition of Amy will give the team more support for developing and strengthening those ideas into something actionable. In its previous incarnation, this team walked all over each other because they didn't think in terms of process. If this team can identify and leverage its strengths, it's going to get where it needs to go faster and with better results."

"You've got me convinced," Tony said admiringly as Kate stared intently at her notes. "Just wondering, how are you going to pick it up again tomorrow? Are you worried that people will resist sharing their perspective of their process? You may be asking for some self-sharing that could make people uncomfortable."

"This morning the team talked about assumptions around data. Tomorrow I'll talk about the assumptions we make around thinking, how our preferences for different phases of the thinking process can affect team results, both negatively and positively. Then I'll lay out the process itself. In the past, the self-sharing comes out naturally within that context because everyone wants to get the work done."

"A little self-awareness can go a long way, Kate. Let me just give you one bit of unsolicited advice." Tony paused dramatically, fork still in the air.

"Be aware of yourself in the process as well. How you present the concepts is as important as the concepts themselves. Take your own medicine and ask yourself how your preferences are influencing your perceptions and decisions here. A team is only as great as the sum of its parts—don't forget to add yourself to the mix."

Kate hadn't seen that coming and found herself slightly taken aback. She was careful not to get defensive and smiled back at Tony. "He sees more than he lets on," she thought. Kate discovered that a new glimmer of admiration for Tony had planted itself in her brain.

chapter 4

The Need and the Way Out

K ate rethought her approach during her morning jog at the lakefront. Just telling people on her team how she had seen their preferences for different parts of the breakthrough thinking process playing out would not generate the same impact as if they saw it for themselves. The first step, she realized, was to cultivate their feeling that a change in their approach was necessary. She'd hit them with Alicia's feedback full force.

Everyone was in the conference room already when Kate entered at 8:00 AM. Pumped with endorphins, she was perhaps in a better mood than was appropriate given the news she was to deliver. She opened the conference room blinds and got right to work.

"Good morning, everyone. We've got a pretty full morning ahead of us, so let me get right to it. I spoke with Alicia yesterday and I got a better sense of the problem she's up against. As you know, she was disappointed with what we provided her last year. Specifically, she did not think we were looking at a complete set of data. She had some data from a state survey I don't think was ever considered. That was the first problem. We didn't diverge enough when exploring the facts around Consolidated's business. As we talked about yesterday, we assumed too much."

"Diverge? What do you mean by diverge?" asked Juan.

"Good question, Juan," replied Kate. Seeing an opening, she decided to introduce the first concept about breakthrough thinking. "If we are going to be successful getting some breakthrough thinking for our client, we need to understand a couple of things about the thinking process that will get us the results we are hoping for. The first thing to know is that at every stage of the process there are divergent and convergent phases. Diverging is what we do when we are generating lots of varied and original ideas, options, and even data. Thinking tools such as brainstorming are based on our ability to think divergently."

"Yes, I understand brainstorming, but that's coming up with ideas. What do you mean by diverging on data? There is a limited amount of data to gather, isn't there?" Juan pressed.

"Is there?" asked Damon. "Obviously, we didn't find all the data we needed to for our reports."

"So I'm told," Juan retorted bitterly, "but honestly, I have been doing this type of business analysis for years. I know where to gather data and what data to get. There is not a lot of 'divergent' thinking needed here."

Maya interjected, "I can see your point, Juan, but I think that might also have played a role in our results. Underlying what you said is another assumption. It's the assumption that we already know where to find the answers."

Juan was not accustomed to being challenged by someone so much younger. In spite of himself, he was impressed with her courage. Maya continued, "It sounds like our client is looking for us to go deeper than usual. For us to go deeper, we are going to need to look at different sources for data and even question which data is relevant."

Kate went on, "Deciding which data is relevant is part of the convergent stage. That's the counterpoint to diverging. When we diverge, we are generating. When we're finished generating, we sift through all the possibilities and pick the best. That's when questions and critical thinking kick in—that's the convergent phase. I'm proposing that we be more intentional with our thinking so that we can recognize where we are in the process."

"So you know a process we should be following? Let's get to it then." Elaine was tired of talking. She was out to make something happen.

"Yes, I do. And I'll show you in a moment. But first, you need to hear the rest of the feedback from Consolidated." Kate spent the next fifteen minutes detailing Alicia's feedback.

The faces of the team members showed they were already feeling a bit beaten down. The feedback was stunningly negative. No one had been in a situation like this before. Sitting with the problem was becoming increasingly uncomfortable. The feedback was giving them a clearer picture of their client's situation. They began to see exactly how their previous work had missed the mark.

Kate continued to relay Alicia's feedback. "Besides the data example, Consolidated was not satisfied with our recommendations," she said. "She thought they lacked originality. According to Alicia, they were action steps routinely discussed among leaders at Consolidated. The report reinforced the status quo rather than challenged it. That's not what they hired us to do."

"Did it occur to her that maybe there isn't another course to recommend? Talk about assumptions! Why is she assuming that our recommendations are incomplete?" exclaimed Juan defensively.

"I think she sees the possibility to expand Consolidated's share of the market and was hoping we would offer some direction," Kate responded. "She's looking for a report that helps her shake up the status quo at Consolidated, to change the conversation at the top of the organization."

"It probably starts with the data we collect and the questions we ask of the data," Amy speculated. "If we looked again at the data we collected on Consolidated, I wonder if we might uncover some interesting opportunities. Did she give you any clues as to what she was hoping we'd find?"

"Not at all. My only sense is that she feels something is missing—that there are growth opportunities that haven't been explored. She was looking to us to help. Juan, if there really is nothing beyond what we've already found, we will have to tell her that. But she doesn't strike me as someone who'd ask us to rework this for nothing. And, I have to admit, when I read the report, I could see her point of view. We did not really entertain novelty here. Nothing we recommended challenges the status quo."

Juan shifted in his seat and took a deep breath. The rest of the team seemed ready to accept that things needed to be done differently, but Juan had dug in his heels. "This is it," Kate thought. "The train is leaving the station and he's deciding whether or not to get on board." In that moment, she realized the team was all staring at Juan, whose eyes were fixed on a coffee mug on the conference room table. They were waiting, too.

Internally, Juan was very uncomfortable. He took stock of the situation. In his mind, his work had been disrespected. A less-experienced colleague had challenged his thinking. His expertise and experience had been reduced to "assumptions." He could get up right now and request a new assignment. Or he could see where this would lead.

Forcing himself to break his unrequited gaze with the coffee mug, Juan looked up. Seeing the eyes of his team fixed directly on him made him smile. They understood what he was going through. In that moment, he knew he was where he needed to be.

"OK, so what is this breakthrough thinking process you've been talking about?" he asked Kate. "I have a feeling we need something to kick-start us here."

The gaze of the group collectively returned to Kate, as if watching a ball returned over a net. Sensing the group had reached agreement, Kate stood at the whiteboard and drew four interlocked diamonds. Starting at the top and circling clockwise, she wrote the following phrases, one in each diamond:

- Clarify situation

- Generate ideas

- Develop solutions

- Implement plans

Above these diamonds she wrote the words "Breakthrough thinking process."

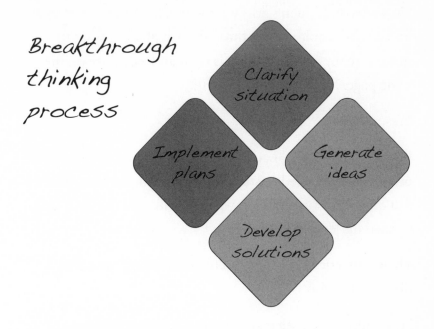

"That's it?" asked Elaine. "We already do that!"

"Of course you do," agreed Kate. "This process simply puts names on the stages of innovation that we all do naturally. There is no big revelation here. The revelation comes in what happens when we consciously follow this process as a team. The power comes in how well we diverge and converge in each phase. And as we reflect on how we work together, you might find that we all approach this "natural" process in a unique way. We all have different preferences when it comes to where we like to spend our time in the breakthrough thinking process. Those preferences will show up when the team works together. Keep that in mind as we move through this, OK?"

"Just a second," Juan said. "On the surface, I think I get this process, but could you go through each phase? I want to make sure my understanding is right and we all are on the same page. No assumptions, right?"

"Yes, please do," urged Amy.

Damon interjected, "Look guys, I get this and I have some other projects I need to stay on top of so would you mind if I just answered some e-mails while we talked about this?" He opened his laptop.

There was a dead silence as all the team members stared blankly at Damon.

"Just kidding...," he recoiled, slowly closing the laptop.

"I can run through this really briefly," Kate assured the team. "'Clarify situation'—this is when you get the data and identify where the real challenges and opportunities are. You start with a long goal. You gather all the data around the goal, diverging on data collection, like we've discussed. After you converge on the key data, you can focus in. You're basically taking the necessary steps to figure out which problem or problems to solve. If people skimp at this step, they end up ..."

"Solving the wrong problem," Amy said, nodding.

"Exactly. Then there is 'generate ideas,'" Kate continued. "Once again, this stage has a divergent and convergent phase. First you stretch for as many ideas as you can. Then narrow them down to a few choice ones. The common mistake here is to dismiss ideas too early, while you're selecting. It's very important to retain the novelty of the ideas and concepts that may seem too wacky or unreasonable on the surface. Maybe some won't work right away, but consider what makes them unique. What could you build on?"

Heads were nodding vigorously around the table, so Kate kept going. "Then there is 'develop solutions'. No idea is going to be perfect right out of the gate. Once you have an idea, you really need to examine it—look at all the factors that may work or not work. That is the divergent part of this phase: thinking how we take the idea from good to great. The convergent phase is about deciding how to actually strengthen the idea."

No questions so far, so she finished up. "Last, there's 'implement plans'. Here's where you identify all the ways to overcome resistance, gain support, and put your plan into action. That's the divergent part. The convergent phase is deciding which steps must come first, second, and so on. Then you decide who does what, get started, and see if the solution actually works."

Maya was intrigued. "Yes, I see this. This is exactly what we do. We just never spend time talking about what we're doing or naming which stage or phase we're in. We pretty much plow ahead, but I don't know if we spend the same amount of time in each area of this process. We kind of just go on autopilot, you know?"

"After doing this work for so many years, what would you expect?" Juan asked.

Maya was a little flustered by Juan's remark, unsure if it was a reference to her inexperience. She decided to ignore it. "Just remembering to diverge and converge at every step.... I mean, I've never been on a team that did that."

"Neither have I," said Amy, showing solidarity with her new team member. "I wonder if that's what happened here. I don't know too many people who are comfortable with talking about their own thinking process or even just checking in about where we are or how we have been doing. Most people like to just move on to the next step and assume everyone else is moving in the same direction they are. But if we don't work through this deliberately, you know, do that, uh ... *reflection* I guess is a good word, we won't have as good a chance of getting something creative."

Then Damon made the leap. "I think we need to build in checkpoints as part of our project plan so that we remember to do it deliberately. It could also help us give feedback to each other."

Elaine was confused. "What do you mean?"

"I mean this checking-in process is a form of holding ourselves accountable," he continued. "That might be why we avoid talking about it. I mean we don't exactly like to give each other open feedback."

"I tell you when you've ticked me off all the time," Elaine retorted with a grin.

"Yes, and that's why we love each other. But I mean, open, real-time feedback related to our performance. Nobody likes to make someone uncomfortable by criticizing them, except Elaine, of course." He threw a charming smile right back at her. "We probably avoid talking process because we don't want to be too critical of each other."

Juan asked, "How is talking about process being critical? I mean it's not like we each own part of the process for ourselves alone. We should always be there at every phase."

Damon said, "Sure, that would be ideal. But are we always there together?"

Kate interjected, "Probably not. Most people like to work on those parts of the process they most enjoy. The way you work together can often dictate who does what and how much time you spend in each of these phases."

"Exactly," Damon continued. "I'll give you a for-instance. Elaine, you've told me that I come up with too many ideas and I need to focus more. Fine. But if we're at a divergent part of this process, coming up with ideas might be exactly what we need to do. Rushing us away from that might be counterproductive."

Elaine could see his point but still felt self-protective. She challenged Damon. "And when I see you disengage from the parts you don't like to do, like, say, putting the project plan together . . ."

"You should call me on it," Damon interrupted. "You're right. That's not where I like to spend my time."

"Fill us in, Damon," teased Maya, "What happens to you when it's time to put the plan into action?"

"I leave that to those who like to do it. They seem pretty good at it and happy to take it over. So I let them," said Damon.

"To be honest, I kind of do the same thing," Juan concurred. "Elaine takes the lead on implementing the plan, so I just back off." Juan looked at Kate to get some recognition for his sharing but Kate did not return his gaze.

"I like to develop and implement plans, too," Maya piped up. "Elaine, I'll help you, even if these guys won't!"

"I appreciate that, Maya. But Juan, I don't understand. You aren't an idea person," said Elaine.

"What do you mean? I come up with lots of ideas!" Juan bristled a bit, feeling as if he had to prove his value to the team.

"No, I don't mean that you don't contribute. You tend to come up with a few really targeted ideas, but I don't see you rattling off one after another."

"Like me," Damon smiled.

"I guess I just feel that once you have an idea that works, why bother with getting more? Use the one that makes sense. That's what I do." Juan struggled a bit with his words. He was really ready to move on to a new topic but thought he better complete this so his new leader wouldn't think poorly of him. "I like to really get into the problem or the idea and play with it. I like to try options to see what happens rather than starting fresh with every new idea. Too many ideas are cumbersome. But what does being a prolific idea person have to do with not being a planner?"

Juan was clearly still feeling defensive. Kate thought his patience for this process discussion was reaching its limit.

"Oh, I see. You like to be in the clarifying or developing phases. Not the ideating or implementing phases. I get it," Elaine said.

"Are we done with this yet?" Juan began to unravel. "What difference does all this make to the bottom line anyway? Sure, we all like different parts of the process. So what? We have a job to do and we all know what that is. Let's get to work! How much more self-reflection do we need to have here?"

"Juan . . . ," Elaine started, concerned her friend was losing his composure, but Juan plowed through.

"I mean, so we all have preferences for different parts of the work process. We also have a client expecting us to come up with something more for them and we have yet to figure out how to give it to them. Kate, I know you mean well here, and it may be that I'm just not used to your approach, but when are we going to get some work done?"

Kate had seen it coming. She had watched the steam inside Juan begin to boil and it had just cleared the pot.

"Juan, my approach is that if we don't spend some time talking about process, we are bound to repeat the same mistakes we made last time." Kate's tone was calm but firm. "If we don't recognize underlying factors that get in the way of good decision making, such as time pressure for a solution, we may unknowingly shortchange steps in the process."

The room was quiet. Juan looked at the floor. The team looked at Kate, Juan, the table.

"Let me press pause for a minute," said Kate. She needed to switch gears and move on. "I've heard a few things in this conversation that are worth thinking about more in depth and I want to capture them so we don't lose them."

On the whiteboard she wrote the following:

1. Talking about process is a form of holding each other accountable, which can be uncomfortable.

2. People lead with their preferences.

"I would add one thing to that second point," Amy spoke up. "It sounds like if you are unaware of process, your preferences might allow you to skip parts. If you don't want to personally do something, you might either let someone else do it or push someone through the process too quickly."

"OK, how about this?" Kate added to the whiteboard:

3. Awareness of process is self-awareness.

"Deep," said Damon. "Who thought we'd get deep?"

"Yes. And one more," said Kate.

4. Without self-awareness, we are more likely to repeat the mistakes of the past.

"So if I follow the logic path correctly: without awareness of process, we are going to submit the same report we submitted last time with the same result. Got it," Juan added, as his eyes stared out the window toward the lake. At that moment he felt as if he were swimming in deep water without land in sight. Things were so abstract. He really wanted something concrete to get a start on the work ahead.

"Yes, Juan. Exactly," Kate acknowledged. "Maybe this is a good place to stop for today. You've all got some work before the weekend and I'll give you a chance to mull over these ideas."

"Kate, I have to admit, I'm kind of with Juan on this one. It feels as if we haven't done anything," said Elaine, her own frustration coming through loud and clear.

"Still trying to get us to implement something, eh?" Damon casually ribbed her.

"Don't worry, Elaine. This is part of the process as well, kind of an underlying method. You guys need some time to let these concepts sit with you. I'd just like to ask you to think more deeply about which parts of this process you enjoy and which parts you'd rather not be bothered with. Review what we've talked about on your own and then get away from it for the weekend. Let it steep in your mind and then ask yourself, 'What implications does this have for how we move forward?' Try to be as concrete as you can when you answer this question. When we meet again on Monday, we'll be able to move a lot more quickly toward applying this stuff."

For a group accustomed to working backbreaking hours and not stopping until the job was done, this approach was new. Elaine and Juan were still antsy but the others felt relief. Juan was clearly frustrated as he left the room amid subdued exchanges: "Have a good weekend." "See you Monday." The group disbanded and Kate was alone with her thoughts.

She remembered the last group she had led. They had been the same way at the beginning. "Once you learn the process, you can learn to trust it," she said aloud to the conference table. The table had heard it all by this time and offered no response.

She smiled, twirled her flip chart marker the way a drummer twirls a drumstick, and gathered her notes to debrief with Tony.

chapter 5

Thinking About Thinking

K ate met Tony at his regular table in the rooftop restaurant. She ordered a salad and an iced tea while Tony, who again had already ordered without her, took a bite of his seared tuna entrée.

"I can't get enough of the fish here. You know, they fly it in daily?"

"Yes, I've heard that."

"So how's that team of yours doing? Anybody quit yet?" he asked with a mischievous grin.

"No, nothing like that. They have actually been pretty open. I think the pain of Alicia's feedback had an impact. They are definitely willing to doing things differently. And they're starting to have some pretty deep realizations."

"Even Juan? He's never struck me as someone with too much patience for 'deep realizations.'"

"Hmm . . . yes, there may be some challenges there. He's been active in the discussions but he gets frustrated when we talk about stages of the process where he's not comfortable. At least, that's how I'm reading it," said Kate.

"The guy's brilliant and maybe a little set in his ways. He's just not used to being uncomfortable."

"I'm not sure what to do with him yet. There are a lot of dynamics going on in this team. Elaine and Damon have this love-hate relationship and I'm not sure how grounded it really is. They kid each other but what's underlying is still a mystery. Clearly, they have a history."

"They've both worked here for years. I would imagine their paths have crossed several times. Do you think the way they are together is disruptive to the group?"

"Not yet," admitted Kate. "Actually, if anything it's been kind of nice. So far they've been a good example of how two people of different types can still work together."

"You may want to point that out. I imagine they could stand with a few compliments at this juncture as well," suggested Tony.

"Good point. Morale is approaching dead low. And adopting new ways of working after you've been comfortable for so long isn't easy." Kate thought for a minute. "I've been focused on getting them to the point of really wanting to change—revealing the need and showing them a new way to see things. I haven't spent time helping them focus on what they do well."

"Don't let that go for too long. It'll bite you in the end," Tony began. "Let me tell you a story."

Kate was making a note to focus the energy on positive attributes of the team when her salad arrived. After one bite, she realized that it was the first time she had eaten that day. She was famished. Fortunately, Tony was feeling talkative, allowing her time to devour her salad like a tornado politely inhaling a haystack.

"Many years ago when I was just starting with the firm," Tony continued, "I was working with a team in Buffalo. We had a client that was pretty demanding, so fourteen-hour days were the norm, and this went on for week after week. Our boss was this guy who really liked the sound of his own voice. So between the two—client and boss—we were all just trying to survive."

"The boss liked to try to come across as if he were trying to help us learn how to do things better, and we'd go along with him. We really didn't see any other choice because ultimately this guy was going to make or break us. My teammates and I were all new to the company, and he had been there for a lot longer, so we didn't feel like we had much power. He'd behave as if he were our professor or something." Tony took another bite of fresh tuna. "After a while, we realized that other than managing the client, which consisted of them partying every other night, he didn't do much work. He was the face of the team and happy to take credit from the client or his superiors, but from our perspective he was only looking out for his own interests. As you can imagine, we began to resent this. Whatever he was trying to teach us just got lost in the shuffle. It became noise that we had to endure just to get the work done."

"Noise? That's pretty harsh," Kate said.

"Not if you were there. Not only was he not getting his hands dirty and helping us produce something, he was always on his soapbox. He'd find something we did wrong and then impart some great wisdom from the mountaintop. After a while, we learned to tune him out, like a nagging parent. He started sounding like the teacher in *Peanuts*."

"Wha wha wha blah wha," said Kate, mimicking the teacher from "You're a Good Man, Charlie Brown."

"Exactly. We got the work done and then every one of us requested a new assignment on a different work team. We couldn't stand it any longer. I still see some of the guys I worked with back then, and we still share those battle scars. In some ways it was a defining moment for us personally but it did no good for the firm. Not long after, we lost that client. Our old boss was hung out to dry."

"Really? He was that bad? What happened? Did the client complain about him directly?" Kate asked, taking a breath between bites.

"No, that wasn't the straw that broke his back. It got worse. He'd make decisions without consulting people. He'd lecture on and on, trying to impress us with his experience and intellect. He'd point out every mistake we made and get upset if he wasn't getting what he wanted. He was a real piece of work. Eventually, he was let go because no one wanted to work with him. I just remember all that ego and self-importance. If any of that ego was earned by expertise, that expertise wasn't missed when he left."

"How sad. Where did he end up?" asked Kate.

"Not sure. I heard once he got into an executive role in a manufacturing company. Maybe he learned from his mistakes."

"And you think I can learn from his mistakes, too?" Kate knew there was a point to Tony's story. He didn't waste time reminiscing about the past for the sake of nostalgia.

"Its great to bring folks this breakthrough thinking process, Kate. Especially, when you see its promise. But you've got to meet your people where they are. If you want them on your side, they have got know in their gut that you're on their side." Tony paused for moment. "Think for a second about a leader who really made a difference to you. How did he or she treat you? I mean, personally."

Kate thought a moment. She remembered volunteering at the local women's center some months back. The director was someone she really admired. She would have worked for that woman forever.

"Yes, I can think of someone right away. She knew me as a person and she let me know her. When there was something that needed to get done, we knew we could count on each other." Kate thought further. "She always made me feel that what I brought to the table was worthwhile. I learned a lot from her and never once felt lectured to."

Tony smiled. She got it.

Kate's thinking went back to the breakthrough thinking process. She remembered her early days with the firm. "You know, now that I think about it, another team leader comes to mind. My first team leader with the firm had this irritating knack of letting me struggle a bit when I'd get stuck in the throes of doing something, you know? She would never step in and do what needed to be done for the sake of speed. Instead, she would talk me through it."

"How would she talk you through it, Kate?" Tony was looking intently at her as if seeing something new emerge from a fog, its features not yet distinct.

"She'd ask me questions about what I've done, what's worked. And then she'd ask me about the next steps. Occasionally, she'd help me summarize something I'd done. Like once when I was working on a project and had this great idea I was implementing that just wasn't working out, she asked me about why I thought it was such a great idea. Where was the data to back up why the idea solved the problem? Where was the planning for getting support for the idea? I could immediately see where I went wrong. I had to go back to the start, which I hated to do. But it was better than beating my head against a wall trying to get an idea working that no one saw any value in."

"Good story," Tony said. "Now let me challenge you a little. How does my leadership story about balancing work and ego and your leadership story about helping others open their eyes to process relate to where you are with your team right now?"

Kate was silent for a long while. Her blue eyes wildly searched the table as if something was there a second ago and had mysteriously vanished.

Suddenly she looked up into Tony's waiting gaze and said, "Juan."

chapter 6

Mapping a Minefield

T he weekend went by quickly, and too much of it, in Kate's opinion, was spent thinking about work. Kate reflected on the way she had been with the team so far. Seeing lots of room for improvement on her part, she developed a plan to meet with Juan first thing Monday morning prior to the team meeting.

Juan came in early as usual, arriving at 7:30 AM. Awaiting him was an e-mail from Kate asking to meet at 9:00. "This is it," he thought. "I'm going to be the first head to roll. Son. Of. A. Bitch."

He spent the next hour backing up his computer, seething with rage. Kate knocked on his door precisely at 9:00.

"Hi, Juan," she smiled as she entered the room. Seeing the expression on Juan's face, her smile quickly vanished. She didn't know much about auras but she would have sworn his was jaundiced yellow, poisoned by depression and angst. Sitting with his arms crossed, staring at his laptop, he seemed to be in midgrowl as she entered the room.

"Uh-oh," escaped her lips accidentally.

Juan pretended not to hear. "Hi, Kate," he said. "What can I do you for this morning?"

"Are you all right? You look like something is really bothering you," she said.

"Let's not play games, shall we? I know what this is about," countered Juan.

"What do you mean? I just wanted to talk to you before our team meeting. I need your help with something."

"You need my help? With what? How to fire me?" he shot back.

"Fire you? Goodness, Juan, is that what you've been thinking? Where did you get that idea?"

"Look. You've made it pretty apparent that we haven't been doing well as a team. You've been lecturing us about how uncreative we are—and me in particular. The data we collected was my responsibility, and although my performance was thorough by my standards, it clearly didn't meet yours. I figured that your request to meet with me this morning was nothing short of a chance for you to have 'The Talk.'"

"Juan, I am so sorry. I realize the feedback I have given the team has been difficult to take. It's been difficult to deliver as well."

"If it was, you certainly did not show it."

"Frankly, I thought it best to just be straight with you," said Kate. "That's how I would like to hear a difficult message. But if I have come across as singling you out, then I did not do my job well. It was not my intention to put you on the spot."

Juan was surprised. From the look of concern on her face and the guilt in her eyes, he began to see she was telling the truth. He had attacked her from his assumptions, not from reality. He had just committed unjustifiable verbal manslaughter of his team leader.

"Uh-oh," he murmured. "What is this about then?"

"I wanted to talk with you about the data. I thought if we worked together prior to our team meeting, we might be able to get some work done and bring it back to the group. I thought it might really save us some time. But maybe I was mistaken. Do you need some time?"

"You wanted to go through the data again?" Juan asked incredulously.

"No, not redo the work. I thought you would be the best person to think about how we might diverge with the data. I want the team to help with the convergent part. With your knowledge of data collection, I thought we could get the work done fairly quickly."

Juan paused again, still finding his legs in this alternate universe. His subconscious was running along the shaky lines of, "Is there gravity and oxygen here? Do atmospheric conditions support life in the form of Juan Esteban Alvarez?" He finally spoke.

"Like I said on Friday, 'diverging,' as you call it, is not one of my greatest strengths. Why would you choose me?"

"Diverging may not be your favorite, but clarifying is clearly a strength. I thought we could combine forces and tackle it together. You see, I'm not much of a clarifier but I actually have a very simple tool that might help us find data we hadn't considered before. I am sure that you're the right person to help if you're willing."

Juan was intrigued, relieved, and a little embarrassed by his assumption of his own demise at the firm. He thought it best to move on quickly.

"Please forgive me. My assumptions seem to be getting in the way again. I'm willing to give your tool a shot. Besides, we'd finally be getting to work."

"Before we do, can I ask a favor?" Kate spotted a learning moment. "Instead of leading with an assumption, can you try asking a clarifying question?"

"What do you mean?"

"Instead of getting all worked up that I might fire you, send back an e-mail saying you're just wondering what our meeting would be about. There's no reason to get all worked up. Seek to understand rather than assume you know the answer."

Juan thought for a moment. "I guess this is the kind of awareness we've been shooting for, huh? OK. I'll try to be more aware of when I am making an assumption and try to ask more questions when I catch myself. Now what about this tool; will we have time to use it now? It's forty-five minutes till the team meeting."

"Let's see how far we get. Have you ever heard of mind mapping?" asked Kate.

"Sounds familiar."

"It's a tool for organizing your thoughts while brainstorming. It helps you see the whole picture so you can find new areas to explore and new connections between the parts."

"And you think we can use it for looking at data? OK. I'm game."

Kate moved to the whiteboard in Juan's office and wrote "Consolidated" in a circle in the middle. "OK, Juan. Tell me about Consolidated. What do we know about it?"

Kate wrote each of Juan's responses around the circle. Then she asked follow-up questions about each. "What do we know about their market share?" "What do we know about their customers?" "What do we know about their products?" And so on. Soon the board was filled with data and lines connecting information to related information.

After about twenty minutes, Kate paused. "OK, Juan, I've run out of space, so let's step back and look at what we have here. Maybe there are a few areas we'll see that we should explore more deeply."

They examined the mess of words and patterns that filled the board. One area, labeled "internal structures," stood out to Kate.

"What if we looked more at how Consolidated is structured toward delivering their products to the customers?" she asked.

"OK. If we do that, I'd also like to get more information about the customers themselves. Who are they really? Are these products really meeting their needs?"

"Good. What else?" Kate asked, holding her own opinions to encourage Juan to present his own.

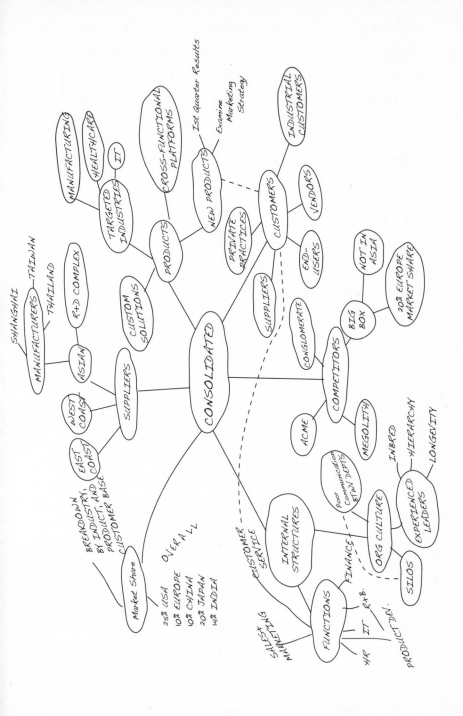

"I was intrigued when we did the original report with this whole area of the marketplace. I'd like to spend more time looking at Consolidated's competitors. We kind of glossed over potential alliances for Consolidated. Depending on the need and the product, there may be room for growth there."

"Great. Let's do that," said Kate with excitement. She could see the process was charging Juan up as well.

Juan put some flip chart paper next to the whiteboard and they dug deeper into areas they found most compelling. Kate wrote "marketplace" on one page. They identified competitors and products. She then wrote "customers" on the other page. They thought about all aspects of the customer, from demographics and income levels to desires and dreams.

After about fifteen more minutes they stepped back again. Some of the customer thoughts matched easily with some of the marketplace thoughts. Some matched with Consolidated's competitors.

"This is great," Juan said. "You can really see where Consolidated stands."

"I think the team is going to love this. There are so many areas to explore."

"Yes. Much more than before," Juan agreed, "but it's still incomplete. Can I have some more time here to play with the map? I think I can add more to this."

"I'm afraid we're going to have to live with incomplete for now," said Kate. "Let's take it to the group and see their reaction. They'll want to add to it. And we'll get their thinking about the best opportunities on this map."

"It's just about time for the meeting. Shall I copy all this down so the team can take a look at it?"

"You know what, Juan? Let's just bring the team in here. They can all fit, don't you think?"

chapter 7

The Power of a Good Question

A fter piling into Juan's office, the team began to take stock of the data. Juan walked them through the mind map. Amy was the first to grab a marker. "May I?" she asked. With a few strokes, she added lines connecting key data points, and new areas to explore emerged. Although Amy and Maya were the most active in the process, Damon and Elaine added their own insights as the mind map branched out. More flip chart paper went up around the whiteboard and the map kept expanding.

Within forty-five minutes, Juan's office wall looked like an office-sized Christo art installation. Damon, whose creativity had shifted into hyper drive, began peppering Juan with rapid-fire ideas.

"Hang on, Damon," Kate cautioned. "Let's try not to leap to solutions too quickly. How about jotting those ideas down so we can talk about them later?"

Kate smiled as Damon made some notes. The team seemed very pleased to be getting into the weeds of the problem. Even Elaine, who didn't much enjoy clarifying, was seeing opportunities emerge from their shared work. Here and there, Elaine would chime in, "There's some low-hanging fruit" or "That area is ready for some work."

As the group slowed down, Kate asked, "So are we ready to start the convergent part of this process?" No objections, so she continued. "Let's get another flip chart pad." Juan stuck a new sheet to the adjacent wall. "OK, guys, where are the natural connections? Do you see any themes here in this map?"

The team volunteered ideas and Juan captured their connections on the flip chart. Kate was surprised that ten different areas of focus emerged. She asked, "Are these all distinct areas?" On reflection, the team grouped three under one common theme and brought two more together under another. That left them with seven distinct areas for analysis.

"Great work, everyone!" Kate said. "Seven areas still seem like a lot."

"Yeah, if we come up with analysis and recommendations for all of them, our report might be several volumes long," Elaine put in. "Of course, we've already covered some of this territory in our previous report. We don't need to focus there again."

Juan spoke up, "We focused on them before because they were important. I don't think we should lose them. Maybe we can use them more creatively later in this process."

Damon said, "There are at least two areas we've never touched—the ones we're calling 'end-user needs' and 'marketplace compatibility.' I think those might lead us somewhere new."

"What do you think we need to do now?" asked Kate. Seeing the team gain independence, she did not want to be too directive here. The team was clearly feeling ownership of the process now that they had some success with the mind-mapping tool. She decided to back off a bit and see where they wanted to head.

"Are we ready to get some ideas on these areas?" asked Damon.

"Ideas about what, exactly?" Juan said. "All we have here are some key areas to focus on; what would we generate ideas about?"

"I agree with Juan," said Amy. "We know what the broad areas are, but they don't offer enough definition for me to think about solutions. I mean, solutions to what exactly?"

Maya turned to Kate. "What do you think? Where in the process do you think we are?"

Kate thought a moment and said, "I think there's one more step we need to clarify the situation. You all touched on it just now: we need something to solve. Juan, thanks for letting us use your office. Let's take a break and reconvene in the conference room in fifteen minutes. Will that work for everyone?"

"Should I order lunch?" asked Maya.

"Great idea. Anyone have any other plans?" In a few moments, lunch decisions were finalized and the team dispersed to check e-mail prior to their next meeting.

Juan and Kate were alone again.

"I have to say, Kate, before you came to my door this morning I had a completely different scenario in my mind of how this day might go," said Juan. "I'm very glad I was wrong."

"Me, too. How'd you think we did?" she said, gesturing at the enormous amount of work covering Juan's office.

"I think we got more done this morning in less time than we usually would. Much less. I'm looking forward to keeping it going."

"Glad to hear it. Me, too. When we reconvene, we're going to diverge a little bit more but in a different kind of way. I think you'll find it interesting."

The group arrived at the conference room one by one. Elaine was first, followed closely by Kate and Amy. Maya and Juan came in next. Damon was late. They started without him.

"This morning we outlined several topic areas to address but we need more specific directions on where to focus. It may seem counterintuitive, but right now, it's time to diverge again. This time, our challenge is to come up with a whole list of angles and perspectives on each topic area. Then we can converge on the framing that really gets to the heart of each topic. It's a good set-up for brainstorming ideas later."

As if on cue, Damon entered the room. "Ideas? Oh good, I've been waiting for this."

"Questions first—then ideas," warned Elaine, fixing Damon with a pointed look that stopped just shy of a glare.

"Drat. All right, hit me with the questions."

Kate continued, "Here's the thing: I'd like you to phrase the questions a particular way. We are looking at getting more deeply into the problem areas that we identified in the mind map. So we're going to phrase our questions using a couple of 'statement starters' that will set our questions on the right path. To help you out, I've written four different statement starters on the whiteboard." Kate pointed to four statements neatly written in a block letters: 'How to . . . ,' 'How might . . . ,' 'In what ways might . . . ,' and 'What might . . . .'"

"Why do you think we are going to do this in this way?" she asked.

No one moved an inch. They looked at her with as much sentience as five blobs of pizza dough. Something clearly didn't connect. Kate decided to wait them out. She let her question float. To amuse herself, she began counting in her head to see how long it would take for pizza dough to grow vocal cords.

By the time Kate counted to seventeen, the blob that was Damon spoke up first (as usual, thought Kate).

"We want questions because they become things to solve?" he asked tentatively.

Kate's blue eyes sparkled with relief at Damon. "Yes—we use open-ended questions that invite lots of possibilities and solutions. She scanned the flip chart and picked a topic. "If we're working on marketplace compatibility, for instance, what might be an issue?"

Maya spoke up. "Other companies in the marketplace may not want to work together."

"Great. And how might you phrase that as a question, using 'How to ...' or 'In what ways might ... ?'"

"Hmm," Maya said, pausing to think. Kate bit her lower lip to keep from answering for Maya. "How about ... ," Maya started, and paused again "... in what ways might we reduce competition? Or maybe, how to work effectively with other businesses?"

Kate wrote Maya's questions on the whiteboard.

Damon burst in like a racehorse breaking the gate. "In what ways might we merge with other businesses? How might we target new markets? What other products do we have that could fly in those markets?"

"Whoa, whoa. Use the stems, please," Kate directed.

"OK. What might be some new markets for existing products?"

"Exactly. You got it," Kate said with genuine enthusiasm.

"How to open doors to new markets?" added Juan, quite pleased with himself.

"How to build alliances with competitors?" added Maya.

"Isn't that the same as your last question?" asked Juan.

"Doesn't matter, let's just get as many questions as possible," advised Kate.

The questions began to flow:

> "In what other locations might Consolidated branch out?"
>
> "How might Consolidated better leverage its global presence?"
>
> "How to shrink in some markets to better grow in others?"
>
> "What might Consolidated do to make itself more distinctive?"
>
> "How to identify the best target markets?"
>
> "In what ways might the market react to Consolidated's change of approach?"

"In what ways might we build trust with strategic partners?"

"What might be possible new extensions to existing products?"

"In what ways might we connect the changes in the marketplace with the way things have been?"

"How might the new marketplace affect current business practices?"

And on they went until Kate had covered three flip chart pages with questions.

As the group's questions slowed to a trickle, Kate checked in to be sure they were still on the right path. "Do you think we have enough areas to explore to meet our goal of providing new directions for Alicia and Consolidated?" she asked.

Reminding them of their goal at this point proved key. The group was gently brought back from the divergence blitz to refocus on their expected outcome. They immediately reviewed their list with a critical eye toward the directions it offered. Was it indeed enough?

"Some of these questions kind of go together," said Amy.

"Yes, I see that, too," Juan added. "But even with that, if we were to pursue all these directions, I think we'd overwhelm our client."

"And it would take forever and a day to complete a new report. We'd need a lot more resources to get it done," added Elaine.

"I don't think we need to start from scratch. Our last report contained a lot of the data we need to explore some of these questions. I bet if we targeted the ones we felt had the most promise, we'd be able to fit it into our existing work," suggested Juan.

"What criteria are we going to use to make that choice?" asked Amy.

"I don't know, you guys; there is one question that just stands out to me. I think if we did nothing else but explore *that* question, we'd be giving Consolidated the creative solutions they're looking for," added Maya, speaking unusually softly, without her typical full-steam-ahead brio. She was sure of her opinion but less sure as to how the more senior members of the team would react.

"I think I know the question you have in mind." Amy's wheels were turning. "Should we just vote?"

"Vote?" asked Juan. "How's that supposed to work?" Juan was skeptical of a democratic process at such a top-driven firm. He expected Kate to make the call.

"Why wouldn't it work?" Kate said. "Do you expect me to be the decision maker of this team? Is that the way I've been behaving?" Kate smiled at Juan. She knew where his reaction was coming from. She also knew she had to call him on his thinking to build trust with the group. They needed to trust in her leadership style as well as trust in the process. Juan was almost there; he just needed gentle reminders.

Juan smiled back. Everything that had occurred this day was very new to him but he was beginning to take it on faith. "No. Certainly not. Forget I said anything. How do you want to vote? Raise hands? A ballot perhaps?"

Damon took the lead. "No, I've done some group voting before. We can do it much easier than a ballot box." "Let's just go up with a marker and draw a check mark next to the question we feel provides the best direction to give Alicia what she needs."

"Yes," said Kate, "I've done something similar. But let's each select three to five questions. I don't want to lose a good one just because someone didn't want use her one vote on it."

"Please, just three—let's get to a decision." Elaine was trying to be patient with the process but sometimes her need to get to the finish line overtook her better judgment.

Damon was pushing her. "Ah, let's just split the difference. Let's go with four."

"All right, fine. Four! But let's get to it quickly." Elaine agreed just to get this group moving—she didn't care where to at this point. Let's go already! she thought. Do I need a cattle prod to get these guys going?

Each person stood and approached the list of questions. When they were ready, each put a check next to the question he or she thought met the client's need best. At least two markers seemed to be moving at once. Within five minutes, there were checks dotting the page but two questions clearly generated the most interest.

"There you have it," Juan said. "Looks like we have a winner or two."

"'In what ways might we connect the changes in the marketplace with the way things have been?' and 'In what ways might the market react to Consolidated's change of approach?'" Kate read. "Any arguments for choosing a different question?"

No one wanted to argue. Kate thought that "arguments" might have been a poor choice of word on her part, so she rephrased. "Does anyone feel strongly about another question up here? If you do, now is the time to make your case. Let's talk about it."

Maya gathered her courage and spoke up. "The one I was talking about before was the question about building alliances within the marketplace. It only got two votes but I still think it's the best. If we look at those other players out there we may be able to combine products or services that would make a huge difference, both in terms of lessening burdens on both companies by sharing costs as well as providing more comprehensive customer experience—you know, a better product delivered more easily. I think if Alicia is looking for something creative, recommendations we can make in regards to alliances around products may be just the thing."

"Thank you, Maya. Well said. Reactions?" Kate asked.

"I think I'm going to change my vote," Damon said, getting up and grabbing a marker. He crossed out one of his earlier check marks and put one on Maya's favorite.

Maya smiled, validated.

"I think Maya is onto something. We didn't look at how to leverage competitors in our previous reports. I think we were in the mind-set that we were out to put them out of business," Elaine added. "That may have been too aggressive a view. I kind of like the idea of looking at ways to partner with them rather than merge fully. I'm changing my vote as well."

And with that short discussion, the question of "How might we build alliances in the marketplace?" supplanted "In what ways might we connect the changes in the marketplace with the way things have been?" as a favorite.

Juan spoke: "I feel good about these two questions. Obviously, anticipating changes in how the market reacts to Consolidated's changes has to be done once we have some recommendations about what those changes may be. Let's just work on that first one—building alliances—and see where it takes us."

Elaine was excited. "Yes! Let's go with that."

chapter 8

From Wild to Workable

After setting aside all their work with questions to be revisited later, Kate wrote the question, "How might we build alliances in the marketplace?" on the top of a fresh sheet of flip chart paper stuck to the wall. She then asked Juan to put the completed mind map from his office up on the opposite wall. "So if we need to look at the data again, we have it. Especially important, let's keep in mind data related to products and competitors. Now before we begin, is everyone clear about the question? Maya, do you want to add anything related to context here?"

"I just want to be sure we all understand what I intended by the question. I mean, we kind of discussed it before but it might be worth saying again just to be sure we are all still on the same page." Her team nodded encouragement to continue.

"What I see is that Consolidated not only produces some great products but also that their products naturally fit with other products out on the market. Some have direct competitors—products that are similar in function—and others are used by their customers in combination. I think we can find ways to generate both cost savings in terms of production and higher profits by looking at how to work with other companies to create more value for the customer."

"Well said, Maya," Elaine added. "You have been doing your homework. This makes a lot of sense to me. I think if we can find some real opportunities here, Alicia should be very excited."

"Let's do this!" Damon said, ideas ready to pop out of his head like popcorn.

"OK, let it out, Damon," Kate said good-naturedly.

Damon rattled off about five ideas faster than an auctioneer on triple-shot lattes. Kate, writing on the board, could hardly keep up. Juan added one. Then Maya had her turn. After about five minutes, Kate was three ideas behind and her forearm was cramping.

"Hold on, guys, hold on. This process isn't working for me. I can go to the gym if I want a workout." She paused and then continued, "Instead of me being the group scribe, I know a way that will help us go faster because I won't slow down the flow by writing. Juan, would you mind finding us enough large sticky notes for everyone to have his or her own pad? Everyone needs to find a pen if you don't already have one."

Juan was back quickly with six pads of sticky notes and some extra pens. Kate began again. "This time, you all are going to do the writing. This way I can just collect the sticky notes and put them up on the flip chart. You can also write the ideas down without having to wait for someone else to be done. You can write them without fear that I might paraphrase on the flip chart to save time. The thing is, when you hand them to me you need to say the idea out loud so everyone can hear it. If you don't say it out loud, I'll remind you. If you have several ideas—*Damon*—I'd like you to say them out loud and pause in between ideas so everyone can hear them individually."

"All right, are we ready to go?" Kate read the question one more time and then began gathering ideas. The amount of ideas generated in five minutes easily tripled over the write-on-the-board method. Over half of a full page of flip-chart paper was now covered in yellow sticky notes and all Kate needed to do was collect them.

Damon came out with one—his fifteenth, by Kate's count. "They could buy a share of FedEx to get a break on shipping costs."

"Oh, come on," Elaine objected. "There is no way FedEx will agree to that!"

"Yeah, Damon. Come back to earth," added Juan. "That's ridiculous."

"Ridiculous? Who are you to say it's ridiculous? You guys wanted some innovation, right?"

"It's not really innovative if you can't use it, right?" Elaine added.

"Hold on, guys," Kate interrupted. "We can avoid this. Just a second." She opened her laptop and typed "brainstorming guidelines" into her search engine. Almost immediately there on the screen was the reminder she needed.

"Juan," she asked, "Would you please write these guidelines on another flip chart sheet?"

Juan found himself happy to help. He was struck that he hadn't felt this way when coming up with ideas in quite some time. Usually he'd become more of an observer when his team was generating ideas but now he felt engaged in the process. He chose a purple marker and began writing as Kate spoke.

"Number one: *Defer judgment.* This means you need to hold off on your judgment while brainstorming. There will be time for critical thinking later on.

Number two: *Get as many ideas as you can.* If you have more ideas to choose from you would be more likely to find ones that work.

Number three: *Allow for novel thinking.* When generating ideas allow for original, even unusual, connections and options. The so-called wild ideas create levity, spark new thinking, and sometimes can be transformed into workable solutions.

Number four: *Look for combinations.* Try to put ideas together to create something new."

"You guys just violated the first guideline," Maya pointed out.

"So there!" Damon added, unsuccessfully attempting to sound like he was joking.

"But that idea was ridiculous!" Elaine couldn't let it go. "I mean, if it's not going to work, and it's obviously *not* going to work, why put it up there? Seems like a waste of time."

It was clear they were not going to get back on track right away. Kate made the conscious choice to deal with the discontent now to avoid such trouble later. They would get back on track after they sorted through their current frustrations. So she asked a question designed to get these feelings out in the open. "Damon, how did it feel when your idea got trashed just now?" asked Kate.

Damon thought for second. "It felt like, 'why bother?' I mean, I'm not going to stop coming up with ideas, especially ones people don't like right away, because that's just who I am. But I did kind of feel like it wouldn't matter. I mean why keep putting things out there if they are going to just get shot down?"

"Maya. You saw immediately how they did not follow the first guideline. How did that make you feel?" Kate asked.

Maya was somewhat embarrassed at being singled out. But seeing in Kate's eyes that she was not going to move on without an answer, she considered things for almost a full minute. Finally, Maya reached into her pocket and pulled out a crumpled yellow sticky-note. She read aloud.

"'Consolidated can invest in its own shipping concern to mitigate costs.' I wasn't going to say anything after the way they reacted to Damon's idea," she admitted.

"Hey, that's actually a workable idea. They could just own a share in the company that they use for all their shipping and provide them all their business. They might end up making back some of their money by just doing what they were going to do anyway. It's basically the same as Damon's idea, just without naming the shipping company," Amy reasoned.

"So you see," Kate said, "one sure way to limit the innovation of a team is to publicly judge each other's ideas."

"Wow. You really weren't going to share that?" Elaine asked Maya, feeling as if she had squashed a child's dreams. She had no idea that her reactions would limit the team's effectiveness to the point of actually preventing a team member from contributing. "I guess I don't realize how I can come across sometimes. I forget people don't all have skin as thick as I do. I'm sorry."

"Was that an apology or an insult?" asked Damon. "People should have thick skin like you? What's that supposed to mean?"

The daily sparring between Damon and Elaine, like two tectonic plates clashing underground, was finally coming to a head. Unchecked, a volatile eruption was certain. Although it clearly made others on the team uncomfortable, Kate let it happen, thinking that if there wasn't a release of pressure soon, worse damage might result. *Look out*, she braced herself, *they're gonna blow!*

"It was an apology, of course," Elaine bristled. "I just mean that I sometimes forget that people can be so sensitive."

"There you go again!" Damon blurted out. Kate secretly wondered what took him so long. She admired his usual tolerance and jovial spirit but Elaine had clearly hit a nerve.

"Look, Elaine, it's not up to people to develop a thicker skin; it's up to you to be more aware of yourself. That's what we have been talking about the last couple of days—about how we need to be aware of how we tend to be. Am I right, guys?"

He waited for the rallying cries of support from the troops. None came. Some inwardly agreed with him but they wanted to avoid the conflict. Instead, as unanimously as if they'd just had a telepathic conference call, all four acted as if the question was rhetorical.

"When we were talking about how we each prefer different parts of the process, that's about who we are, right? I mean, we can't control that. What we can control is how we use those preferences." Damon began to feel slightly guilty, like he was browbeating Elaine publicly. This was contrary to his nature; he knew his frustrations had gotten the best of him in that moment, but once the steam began to vent, there was no stopping it.

"Remember when we were working on the original report, Elaine? I had brought up the shipping issue then and you not only dismissed it, you slammed it. I felt like 'what's the point?' You guys seemed bent on going the same directions we always go. Coming up with something different seemed not just pointless but also just plain unwelcome."

Elaine's self-defense mechanism kicked into full gear. She felt her shoulders tense and her face get hot. She heard Damon and knew he had a point but feeling attacked at that moment she reacted out of impulse.

"At the time, that didn't seem like what the client was asking for. We had a direction and a due date and I was going to make sure we met it. At that point, by the way, I remember you just seemed to check out of the project altogether." Elaine stopped herself abruptly. What had started out as her attacking Damon back, trying to blame him for their collective poor results, suddenly took on a different flavor. Given their conversation, she realized that his energy for the project had diminished because he felt as though his contribution was not valued.

"Oh . . . ," she said haltingly, "I didn't realize that was where you were coming from." It was a moment she would long remember as the time when she saw clearly how her behavior directly affected others. Elaine was embarrassed but composed herself quickly. It was as if she had tripped, fallen, and risen up again in one fluid motion and was brushing herself off getting ready to continue on her way. "It's OK, Damon. You have a good point and I guess I owe both you and Maya an apology. I could have reacted better. I guess I didn't realize that this was the sort of self-awareness we've been talking about."

Kate thought Elaine looked humbled but maintained her professional composure well. That was enough apologizing. It was time to help the group move on.

"Let's just try to be more aware of how we are as we go through the process. For now, let's stay with these guidelines and see what kind of ideas come up. I think you all see the power of the first one, deferring judgment. It's key. Remember, we'll be judging these ideas when we start converging. For now, though, in this phase, every idea is welcome. The wackier the better." She scanned the web page on her laptop detailing the guidelines to brainstorming. "Check out this quote: 'It's easier to tame a wild idea than invigorate a tame one.'"

"Ah, I can see that," said Maya without realizing she said it out loud.

"That's from Alex Osborn," added Kate. "Says here, he's the guy who coined the phrase 'brainstorming.'"

"It makes sense. I mean, if you don't push the boundaries, how are you going to end up with something new?" said Amy, who was happy the conversation was moving away from the "Days of Elaine and Damon" soap opera. "I guess that's what I did with Damon's idea. I mean, Consolidated isn't going to buy FedEx but they could own a few shares of something like it."

"That's exactly it, Amy. Well done. Do we need a break or are we ready to keep going?"

As if on cue, the knock on the door decided for them—lunch was being delivered.

"Break!" the team said, with collaborative smiles all around.

"Perfect timing," agreed Kate. "Let's take ten and come back for some grub."

chapter 9

Combining the Unlikely

T he team reassembled slowly. The tension from the first take at brainstorming was quickly becoming a distant memory as the group refocused on the problems they were there to tackle. Kate was sure not to bring the group back to the activity too quickly. Instead, she encouraged small talk. She wanted to get to know her team a little more personally. They had yet to have that time together, so she started to ask some seemingly benign questions, but in truth, she was very interested in their responses.

Over lunch, she learned that Amy had a toddler in preschool. Elaine's kids were in college—one was adrift on the party circuit with no major in sight and the other (engineering major) just got his nose broken playing rugby but was on the mend. Damon was an artist in his spare time but was a bit coy about what kind of art it exactly was, which Kate allowed to slide. Maya was in a relationship with the same man for the past five years and seeming quite happy together with their two cats, a Birman and a Maine Coon. Juan was an avid carpenter on the weekends and in the midst of remodeling his kitchen piece by piece, much to his wife's frustration.

For her part, Kate revealed that her kids were in high school and her husband, Luke was a marine botanist who explored the muck in all of its corners, from the Everglades to the Galapagos. Luckily they didn't ask her about global warming. She spared them Luke's speech about global warming shrinking oxygen in large sections of the earth's seas, creating dead zones at near-crisis levels. The algae were loving it—the Dungeness crabs not so much. Another example of how crisis can be good for some and not for others.

Once everyone was finished and the lunch debris cleared away, they went back to task relaxed and revived. Kate reminded everyone of the guidelines for brainstorming and they went back to their sticky notes. Between the prelunch brainstorm and the current one, the team depleted their supply of ideas in short order. Within about ten minutes, they had generated over one hundred new ideas. Some were wild, some were not, and some were a combination of ideas already presented. Just as the ideas seemed to be exhausted, there was a knock at the door of the conference room. Tony poked his head in.

"Hey, everyone, how are things ..." his voice trailed off as he noticed the incredible amount of flip chart paper, writing, and sticky notes covering the room for the first time. He smiled, "Hmmm, looks like we got some brainstorming happening here! All right. Nice. Good to see."

"Want to take a look and see what you think so far?" asked Kate.

Kate noticed that Juan and Elaine both seemed a little surprised by her invitation as they shifted in their seats and looked down at their own papers. She realized that it wasn't customary in their firm to share their work openly before it was complete. The others seemed to just take it in stride, caught up in the flow of the day.

Tony perused their work as if he was had just entered an art exhibit. He was first attracted to the mind map. Juan decided to take it upon himself to explain their thinking. Tony would only reply with "Yes, yes, I see. Uh-huh. Interesting."

Then he moved to the wall with their key questions. Damon mentioned they had a lot more and pointed to a pile of flip chart paper filed with questions resting in the corner of the room. "Yes, good," said Tony.

"And these are your ideas so far?" Tony asked.

"Yes. I think that's all of them." Elaine said.

Some of her team noticed again how quickly Elaine liked to put a lid on diverging—even hypothetical diverging—but no one said anything.

"You mean you're done? Looks to me like you're just getting started," pronounced Tony. "Whose handwriting is this? It's all over the place," he said, pulling a sticky note off a chart and showing it to the group.

"That's mine," Damon said.

"I might have guessed, Damon. You've always been one of our best idea guys."

"He's the most creative, that's for sure." Elaine said.

"Really? I doubt that's true. He's the most prolific, for sure. But I bet if I looked at the innovative ideas up here, I'd find plenty from you, too, Elaine."

Elaine shook her head. "No, I'm not all that creative. I can put a plan together and get it done better than anyone but I wouldn't say I'm necessarily creative."

"Really? I bet I know a way to get your creativity flowing and to get you to think about some more ideas. Give me second; I'll be right back." And with that he left the conference room and headed to his office. In a few minutes he returned with a bag from a toy store.

"I was just at the toy store across the street. I had to pick up some stuff for my grandkid's fifth birthday and after this I can write it off as a business expense," he said, smiling.

Confused but curious, the team gathered around Tony as he reached into his bag like Santa on Christmas Day. He pulled out a small, kid-sized basketball, which he flipped to Elaine. Then he pulled out a Rubik's cube. He flipped that to Maya. Last, he pulled out a box of multicolored pipe cleaners.

"These are awesome. You can make anything out of pipe cleaners," Tony said, his face glowing with a child's enthusiasm. He held one up for everyone to see. "OK. Ready to play along? Ready to force yourself to think a bit differently?"

The team nodded in agreement, so he continued, "Kate, would you mind scribing please?"

"Sure thing," she said, jumping up and grabbing a blue flip chart marker.

"What can you all tell me about these pipe cleaners?" Tony asked, passing the pipe cleaner container around the room.

"They're flexible."

"They've got lots of colors."

"They're long."

"They're thin."

"You can twist 'em into different shapes."

"You can tie them together."

"They can fit into tight spaces."

"They are made of wire."

"They're furry."

"Good, good," said Tony. "That's fine. I bet we could come up with some more, but that's a good start. Now let's take one of your descriptors. Amy, pick one."

"You can twist them," she said, picking one of her own.

"Fine. Twist 'em. Think about twisting these pipe cleaners." He took some out and gave a few to each person on the team. "What ideas for 'How might we build alliances in the marketplace?' can you get from twisting?"

"How about finding ways to get multiple pipelines to flow together?" said Damon.

"Get different suppliers to Consolidated to work together to serve them better?" added Maya.

"Partner up with the most flexible competitor," added Amy.

"Build a redundant supply chain," added Juan.

And so the team was producing more ideas, even though they had thought they were done when Tony arrived. With every toy more ideas came.

Some ideas spurred on from the basketball:

"Bounce it off our venders."

"Create a 'Final Four'-type competition for our business."

"Try some free throws—give people an opportunity to work for free."

"Create a league of companies that are complementary."

From the Rubik's cube:

"Align with companies just like ours to shape the market."

"Figure out what customers really want and match up with others to provide the total solution."

"Look for the missing piece—what is Consolidated missing and who has that piece?"

"Find companies with a totally different approach to Consolidated and work together to provide comprehensive solutions."

Tony was clearly having fun and two more flip charts were soon filled with new ideas. "It's not so hard to push for more ideas when you force your mind to make some connections."

"I love this game. Let's do more," Damon said excitedly.

Elaine couldn't help herself. "No, please, don't we have enough?"

"After filling up five flip charts with about sixty ideas on each sheet, I would hope we have enough," Juan said wearily.

"There are several themes I see coming out—there are ideas around our competitors, some around suppliers, some around customers," noticed Amy.

Kate saw the team was already moving to the convergent phase. "Tony, that was great. Thanks for doing that. It sounds like the group is seeing a lot of potential in all these ideas. Maybe we should let them move on and do some critical thinking about them."

"Thanks for indulging me, guys. I remember reading somewhere that the most original ideas generally come at the end of a brainstorming session, after you have pushed yourselves to go beyond the typical brain dump, you know, the ideas you've already thought of that aren't that new. And that's just what you've done. I had fun and I think you've got some very innovative strategies up here. If you select and develop a few of these, I think Alicia will be really pleased."

"Thanks, Tony." The team was grateful and a little relieved to be getting some positive feedback from the boss on their new approach. Kate was impressed that Tony made no judgments about the group's work. He just went with the flow and let the group continue on its path. Not many leaders at his level would show a group so much trust, she thought.

"Just one thing I'd like you to keep in mind as you move forward. As you begin to select the ideas that have the most potential for our client, don't lose the novelty. Just because it sounds a little crazy or unlikely to work doesn't mean everything about it should be completely dismissed." Tony looked each member of the team in the eye as if to make sure they understood that this was a challenge to each of them personally. "And with that, I will take my leave. Great working with you all." The team helped him gather his grandson's toys before he left the room.

"Looks like I'll need more pipe cleaners," Tony said to himself as he closed the door behind him.

Kate turned to the group. "Let's take another break. It's getting kind of late, so if you need to check your e-mail or catch up on things, now is a good time to do it. How about we meet back here in an hour?" Then she followed Tony down the hall to his office.

chapter 10

Be Careful What You Wish For

T ony was very enthusiastic about the team's progress. Kate was as well, but deep down she felt that they were about to enter the part of the process that may have been a stumbling block in their past efforts. They both sat at the small table in the corner of his office.

"Great group of people, Kate. I think you got a lot to work with. I saw some ideas up there I might want to take to some other client teams."

"Thanks, Tony. It hasn't been easy, but I'm pleased with the work so far. They feel the need to do things differently and are willing to try the breakthrough process. I think this next part is going to be critical though."

"Oh?" said Tony, wondering what was coming.

"There are some interpersonal issues surfacing and there will be some logistical issues ahead as well."

"First, logistics. What do you need?" Tony asked. In his mind he was thinking about his own first rule of leadership—clear the way for your people to succeed. If resources were going to be an issue, he wanted to address that right away to enable the team to do its work.

"Like you said, we have a lot of ideas. I can tell that if we are going to be able to develop them, we're going to need some help. My team is talented but we can get the job done faster and better with some help from others in the firm."

"I expected that. I'll talk with the other partners and see whom I can shake loose. Specifically, you want business analysts, correct?"

"Yes. The more the merrier. That and some dedicated administrative support. I think if the team has a plan, they might be able to complete the work in a couple of weeks."

"Consider it done; Consolidated is a big client and I don't think I'll have any trouble rearranging things to bring our resources to bear for a couple of weeks. Now what about the interpersonal issues you mentioned?"

"We've had some conflicts today that I think mostly come from style differences. A couple members of the team can't really hear each other, you know. It's like their point of view is so set, they can't yet see from the other's point of view. I have a feeling these next steps—the developing, the implementing—are going to be the hardest to keep everyone engaged. Earlier, I was able to help them begin to talk about it. I'm just worried people are going to lose patience or just get annoyed by the self-discovery they are going to experience along the way."

"Tell me more."

"Elaine is a great implementer. In fact, pulling her reins back in the early stages of the process was important so that we allowed time to really clarify the situation and come up with some targeted ideas. She'd been really good so far at holding back—self-censoring, if you will. But it has been a challenge for her. Now that we are going to develop ideas, I need to keep her focused on making those ideas strong before leaping toward action steps."

"OK, that's one."

"Damon has been glowing lately because we've been brainstorming a bunch. I think he will be fine with developing at least the divergent part of how to make these ideas stronger but after that, when we converge and strengthen those ideas and when we get to implementation, I think there's a chance he might pull back from the group."

"That's two."

"Juan has really turned a corner today. I think he's totally onboard with the process so far. He's had a chance to really get into the weeds of the issues at Consolidated in ways he had not before. Maybe as a result of that he was able to stay engaged in the ideation sessions. That said, implementation might be a bit scary for him. He'll have to stop exploring and come down to actually getting closure on the project and I hope he'll feel good about it. But I'm worried he might hold us back."

"OK, what about Amy and Maya?"

"Amy and Maya have been pretty much engaged the whole way. In fact, Maya has been really helpful in helping people see things differently. She was essential when we were converging on problems in helping the group focus on something valuable for our client. I hope she'll continue to be able to help bridge different perspectives as we move forward. Amy has also been helpful, especially in clarifying the situation. But deep down, I see her strength as someone who likes to develop ideas. She seems very thorough, very much in the weeds. I have a feeling she might frustrate Elaine in that she'll want to dig deep into the developing part while Elaine will be ready to run on to implementing as quickly as possible. She's a data specialist, you know. Going deep into data and producing results is where she's experienced."

"OK. That's five. Sounds like you can see the players well. How about yourself?" asked Tony.

"I've got to admit, I am focused primarily on the end result at this point and turning our relationship with Alicia around. I want to be sure we blow her away with our best thinking."

"So where in the process are you focusing then?"

Kate thought for a moment. She didn't necessarily enjoy the way Tony was going with his questioning. She would have much preferred to stay focused on getting the team to do what it needed rather than herself. She liked to see herself primarily as a facilitator of the team and not as much one of its members.

"My focus is on them. Getting them to do what we need to do," she replied. "Isn't that what you expect of me?"

"Sure it is, Kate. But if you are going to be able to do that well, you need to recognize that you have your own preferences and they will influence how you work with the group. So I'll ask you again, where in the process do you seem to want to spend your time?"

"Right now, I'm focused on developing, I guess."

"That's what I heard in your descriptions of others. You are concerned that you may be the only one who will want to focus completely on this part of the process."

"Yes, and that's where we need to be in order to make sure we have the best product to win us back this client. I think it's imperative I keep the team focused on the developing part of the process. At the same time, I have to continue to encourage self-awareness of the process. I'm worried I have two places where the group might get bogged down or sidetracked."

Tony looked into her eyes as if he had lost something and knew he would find it deep in her corneas. "Kate, you're the best facilitator I know. You can handle both of those potential problems. What's really got you worried?"

Kate had to look away from his stare, so she stood up and walked to the window. Looking out at the city below she reflected on her anxiety. Cars and trucks maneuvered through the canyons between the buildings below. People scurried about on the streets, madly rushing toward their destinations. Where were they all going? she thought. Then it struck her.

"I think it might be the direction we are heading," she said to the city, still avoiding Tony's stare. "I'm not convinced we're heading the right way, and I've got to be if I'm going to lead them there. You know what I mean?"

"You have a lot of potential directions to go in. That room we were just in is full of directions. Do you mean you're just not sure which is best?" asked Tony from his seat.

Yes, I guess that's it," she said, though that explanation of her anxiety still felt incomplete to her. She turned around and dared to look at Tony again. "In order to lead these people and set them up for success, I need to know we are on the right track. Do you think we are?"

"You know who you should be asking, right? It's not me."

"Yes. You're right. I need to check in with my client. Alicia needs to help us pick which ways we should be going," Kate said, as if it should have been obvious to her.

"OK. Are you ready to have that conversation with her?" asked Tony.

"She's been open to my contacting her before. I think she'll be interested to hear the directions we've been thinking about going."

"Yes. But this conversation will be different than earlier in this engagement—now it's mission critical. You are not simply asking for her guidance on which direction she likes. This conversation is also about laying the groundwork for success."

"Say more," Kate said, intrigued.

"Two things: the first is about helping the client be open to the creativity of the group. She has asked for something creative but it's a case of being careful what you wish for, you know? Is she is really going to be open to creativity? If you present her with some far-out ideas without priming the pump a bit, she is more likely to swat them down and call your efforts a waste of time. How might you get her buy-in for the general direction you are heading—how might you increase the probability that she will accept what the team is generating?"

"And second?" asked Kate.

"The second issue is one of the hardest challenges consultants face. How you keep your client in the client role and not the 'boss' role is critical in this situation. Alicia has asked for our expertise and that is what we have to provide and ultimately sell to her. When you ask for direction, you run the risk of giving her too much control of your team. You are not asking for her approval of specific ideas. You are asking about openness to the direction you are heading. Again, how open to novelty is she really? Her approval is what happens later on when she gets our full report—our analysis of recommendations. This conversation is getting her ready to receive those results. You see what I'm getting at?"

"I think so. I need to check in with her to both confirm our direction and ready her for what might be coming. I get it. That makes sense." As Kate said these words, she was already trying to imagine how this conversation with Alicia might go. She paused in thought. "But what do you mean about not letting her be 'boss'? If the satisfaction of our client is our goal, how can I not see her as the boss?"

"Kate, she hired us for our expertise. She will ultimately decide what the right way to go is. She may hail us as prophets or dismiss us as lunatics. Our job is to bring her our best thinking. If we give her our well-reasoned ideas, we enable her to use her best judgment to decide her course. If we don't, we fail her. If we ask her to make the choice of direction before we've given her our best analysis of both process and steps, then we've done nothing for our client.

Instead we enable her to continue to make the same mistakes. You have to guide her a little now. Get her ready for our directions so she can see them with some positive anticipation rather than killing the novelty she requested."

This made some sense to Kate. As she began to think it through, she again began surveying the city outside the window. After a moment or two seeking to clarify the issue more, she likened it to something else she had been through. "On my last assignment our client was terrific. He was crying out for something new. I never had to worry about whether he would take our direction. He craved it. Alicia is in a different place. She is balancing a lot of expectations and we have to come through with something that will fit those expectations and at the same time challenge them. . . ."

"So you think," Tony came back, "in reality, how she handles what we generate is her work? What you have to manage is your work. What are you going to bring to her and how can you prepare her to hear it?"

Kate nodded. In her heart she was coming to grips with the limitations of her consulting role. She could not tell the client definitively that this way or that was the right course to take. She could only put forth some new directions and help her client understand the thinking behind the proposals. As she looked at the city she noticed the awkward pattern of starting and stopping traffic. She could hear the muffled sounds of sirens and horns from the streets below.

"I'm going to call her as soon as I can, just to get a sense of her openness to the directions we're thinking. Nothing too specific," Kate said. "It will be a conversation that informs us both," she said as she turned her back to the city beyond the windows and refocused on the partner in charge of the account.

Tony smiled. He had an idea what Kate was thinking about and decided to offer one more bit of advice. "Just one thing, for what it's worth: I mean, you probably are already going to approach it like this, but I would lead with some questions. Find out generally if she sees the potential of the idea groupings you've generated. Ask her questions to make your own determination as to whether those are indeed the best directions in which to proceed."

"Exactly where I was going with this. Thanks, Tony, this helped me sort it out. I have some priming of the pump to do," Kate said, "and then I'll feel more confident we are heading down the right path. Thanks for this."

"Good luck, Kate. Keep me posted," Tony said as she left his office and headed back down the hall to the conference room.

Before she walked into the room, she was stopped in her tracks by the noise coming from inside. She could hear two conversations happening with both sets of people trying to talk over each other. She listened for a minute to try to guess what was going on and not interrupt the flow of energy that had taken over the room.

She heard Juan, Elaine, and Amy debating the qualities of different ideas. Damon and Maya seemed to still be generating more ideas. Her excitement over the team's energy quickly turned to anxiety as she realized the team was no longer working together.

chapter 11

Preserving the Novelty

K ate entered the room. "Looks like you folks have been busy. What's going on?"

Damon replied, "Maya and I are still coming up with more ideas. This is really fascinating stuff."

Elaine spoke up. "Ideas? Please. We have enough ideas!"

Juan fixed his gaze on Kate, adding, "We've been seeing how these ideas relate to each other. I think we are seeing some clear patterns emerging."

"Wow. I'm impressed that you are all so ready to get down to the business of converging on what is going to work best for our client. I think you're off to a good start," Kate said, trying to maintain the group's momentum. Then she tried to redirect it.

"Before you go any further, I'd like to remind you all of the last thing Tony said as he left the room earlier—don't lose the novelty. In fact . . ." Her voice trailed off as she moved over to her laptop and typed "convergent guidelines" into her search engine. The team watched curiously.

"Here we are, 'convergent thinking guidelines.' Will someone scribe for me?" she asked. Then, thinking this might be a way to get Damon interested in the next phase, added, "Damon? Would you mind doing the honors?"

"Happy to, Kate."

"Number one: *Be appreciative.* This is about training yourself to first look at what you like about the idea. What about the idea can you appreciate?" Kate explained and then continued.

"Number two: *Be deliberate.* This is about making sure you don't move too fast. Consider each idea individually.

Number three: *Remind yourselves of the goal.* Does this idea or set of ideas hit the right target?

Last one, number four: *Consider novelty.* This is the one Tony was talking about. What about this idea makes it unique? What potentials might come from this idea?"

She looked around the room, unsure if presenting these guidelines put her too much back in "teacher" mode or how her intervention had changed the team's dynamic. She waited to see.

"These are nice guidelines, Kate," Elaine began, "but how do we actually do this? I mean, sometimes the solution is obvious. Are you saying we should go back and check that we've done our thinking around these guidelines?"

"No. These are guidelines to be used as you sort through the ideas you have generated. It's just the same as how you hold each other accountable to the guidelines for divergent thinking while brainstorming. You have to first try to be aware of what you are doing and second you have to name it when you see it. If I think Juan is being too negative toward a particular idea, I might ask him, 'Juan, what do you appreciate about this idea?' That's the kind of support you can give each other during this process."

"And if I see Elaine wanting to move forward too quickly I might say, 'Sit down and shut up,'" Damon laughed. "Come on, Elaine, just kidding! I would say something like, 'Let's try to be deliberate.'"

"That's a little better," Elaine said. "Or you could say, 'Hold on, let's look at this more carefully.' I might respond a bit better to that."

Kate was delighted that Elaine and Damon were laughing at each other again. "Nicely said, Elaine. What is another way you might be able to hold each other accountable to these guidelines as you move forward?"

As she paused, she realized that the group was rolling with her in the role of "teacher" but she knew she couldn't stay in it for long. She needed to jump back into the team as an equal member.

"I could try to make sure the first thing I say is, 'I like this idea because . . .' just to make sure I am in the habit of that," said Maya.

"Thanks, Maya. Any others?" When there was no response, she got the group back to task. "Amy, earlier you said you were already seeing some themes emerge from the ideas on the wall, right?"

"Yes—they are practically leaping off the wall," Amy replied.

"Good. Here's my thought. How about you guys spend a few minutes working together to create the themes. Go ahead and move the sticky notes that seem to fit together into one place. See how many themes emerge. Then using the guidelines, I'd like you to consider which ones fit the needs of our client the best, the ones we should develop further into something that will work for Alicia."

Damon wrote the steps under the guidelines: "first themes, then discuss," and then asked, "Should we rank them? Maybe see which ones we'd give priority?"

"Yes, but don't rank them until you've got your themes together. The process of ranking is another opportunity to apply these guidelines. While you are doing that work, which is really only the beginning of how we converge, I am going to call our client. I want to be sure we've been heading in the right direction. If we are going to use that third guideline, I need to be sure we are on the right path. Is that all right with you guys?"

"Wait—which ideas are you going to tell Alicia? We haven't even narrowed things down yet." Maya was concerned. It made her anxious that they had not yet completed the process.

"Don't worry," Kate began, "I'm not going to present any specific ideas, just check in that our overall direction is something she is open to. I think we also need to get an idea of how open Consolidated is to our novel direction. Sometimes you've got be careful what you ask for and asking for creativity may sound great on the phone but when you see it in real life it can make you uncomfortable at first."

"Ha! Trying to fend off an attack already?" Amy laughed. "I guess they aren't following the same guidelines we are."

"Exactly. It's going to help to prime the pump a little before we give them what they need."

Kate's explanation seemed sufficient. The group let her go and began to self-organize around the work that needed to be done. Kate paused outside the door just long enough to hear Juan say, "This won't be hard. Lots of these fit together."

"When do we use the guidelines?" asked Amy.

"Through the whole process, I think," said Maya.

With a reluctant sigh, sounding like she was agreeing to polish Mount Everest with a toothbrush, Amy relented. "Over here I see a bunch of ideas that seem to go together ..."

Kate continued down the hall to her office, thinking this stage was going to prove interesting. She forced her mind to come back to the crucial call ahead of her. It was time, in Tony's words, to "prime" Alicia.

chapter 12

Priming the Pump

A licia had logged more than twenty years at Consolidated, having started there right out of college. She rose to a leadership role, as she saw it, by using a triple-threat combination of determination, sacrifice, and working harder than everyone else. Coworkers viewed her as a formidable, competent leader and knew that if you presented to Alicia anything even in the hemisphere of "touchy-feely," you were going down. Fast. Tough to please, she expected results first and foremost.

Kate had heard these impressions, too. She had experience working with similar personalities, so as she geared herself up for the conversation she focused on her main talking points, taking notes to keep herself on track. Any casual slips about group harmony could be disastrous.

Here are the objectives she considered:

- Gauge the level of comfort for innovation

- Gauge commitment to improvements—felt need for change

- Assure client we are on the same page and have heard her concerns

- Confirm direction—"How might we build alliances in the marketplace?" Does this make sense to her?

Then, to be sure she had the information needed to meet these objectives, Kate spelled those out as well:

- What does innovation mean to Alicia?

- For Alicia, where is the need for innovation coming from?

- What might be the reaction of her fellow leaders to a new and different approach?

- How has Consolidated explored alliances in the marketplace? What has been the interest thus far in this potential area for growth?

Kate started to think a little more deeply about what she might say that would lay the groundwork for the team's success. She added a couple more questions:

- If Alicia is interested in exploring areas for growth, what might be the biggest barriers for her in getting the ideas accepted at Consolidated?

- Given my firm's latest track record with Consolidated, what might be the barriers to getting our ideas accepted there?

The preparation helped move the focus of Kate's energy from her team to back to her client. She needed to nail this one. She needed to come across as confident but listening well at the same time. The team had been invigorated over the last week by the progress made toward providing something innovative for their client. She didn't want their work to go unnoticed or unappreciated. But all these thoughts were about her and her team's needs—not her client's. She tried to consciously put those thoughts aside.

"Ultimately, this isn't about me," she coached herself out loud. "It's not even about my team and how hard they have worked. It's about the client—what does she need and how can we be helpful?" She dialed the phone number.

Alicia's assistant answered the phone and asked her to hold, allowing a wave of orchestral music to fill up the dead space on the line. "What if she doesn't take my call?" Kate thought with apprehension. "Should I ask everyone to wait till I hear from her?" Fortunately, she recognized the music as the Prozac rendition of "Dude Looks Like a Lady," which made her smile and relax a little before Alicia's voice came on the line.

"Kate, so good to hear from you so soon. What can I do for you?" She got right down to business.

"Hi, Alicia, I just wanted to touch base with you, as my team has been working pretty swiftly at providing something special, something that's going to add some real value to you and Consolidated. In fact, we have been examining a lot of new perspectives and have some new ideas of ways to approach things."

"Great." Alicia sounded as though she wasn't convinced by a long shot—but was willing to play along for now. On the other end of the line, Kate tried not to imagine herself as a mouse dangling from a cat's claws. "How can I help?" said Alicia.

"I was wondering if I could ask you a few questions, just to be sure we are on the right track."

"Of course, go ahead."

Looking at her list of questions, Kate led with her second one, "We have heard loud and clear that you wanted and expected more innovative ideas from us and that has been entirely the direction we've been taking. We'd like to provide some breakthrough thinking that really hits the mark. The last time we spoke you were pretty clear that the same old reports you might expect from a firm like ours weren't going to cut it. We have been up for this challenge, that's for sure, but my team does have some concerns. For instance, can you tell me a little about how receptive your colleagues might be to some real 'out-of-the-box' ideas?"

The smile on Alicia's face sang through the phone. "I would say, frankly, that it will be a challenge for them. As you know, the latest economic news has not been good. We are feeling the strain like everyone else and what I am seeing is a tendency to hold on to the tried and true. In fact, your last report just reinforced that kind of thinking. But what I would like is some new data and some new courses of action that might turn that feeling of desperation, that feeling of just holding your head above water, into one where people feel strong enough to swim." She paused for a moment, considering what she had just expressed. "Yes. The need to do something is there but the desire to move from cautiousness and preservation to something more . . . I don't know the right word . . . exciting? Exploratory? Future based! Yes, that's it, more future-based thinking. But I'm not sure they are ready for that. There's a lot of fear, to be quite honest."

"I understand. What we have been putting together is very much oriented in that direction—future based—and we'll be providing some recommended steps on how to make that future a reality. One of the general categories that we've been thinking about is how Consolidated uses its marketplace. How open do you think people might be to exploring how Consolidated might build alliances in the market?"

Alicia thought for a moment. "I'm not sure we're there yet. I agree it's an interesting avenue to pursue and we might end up finding some great ways to leverage competitors and influence our immediate revenue stream . . ." Her voice trailed off. Perhaps hearing these words in own voice made her reconsider the idea because then Alicia said, "You know, I might be able to socialize that idea before you present it. That might help open some ears."

Kate could not believe her luck. Her client was either flexible and strategic by nature or desperate enough to try anything. Either way, she liked what she was hearing. Alicia was willing to start talking about her team's initial direction, which she hoped would create a supportive environment for their report to land in.

When confronted with something new, Kate understood, people have a tendency to either attack it, run from it, or remain perfectly still. Fight or flight or freeze: the response that we have wired into our ancient brains, along with every other animal in the world. It served us well against saber-toothed tigers but can be very limiting in our daily modern lives. After all, we're confronted with newness constantly—in our e-mail in-boxes alone there's enough new information each morning to give a caveman a stroke. Alicia's willingness to prepare her colleagues for their report would certainly help circumvent the fight-flight-freeze tendency, but would that be enough? Kate followed up with a new question.

"You mentioned the difficulty in the economy and how it's been affecting Consolidated. I'm wondering what is being done to manage the stress that has to be there. Stress can get in the way of accepting new ideas, reinforcing that tendency you mentioned to go back to the tried and true. Novelty is not often welcome when people are under stress."

"I'm not sure stress is something we can control," Alicia said, wondering where this was going. "Times are tough, so stress is going to be there. What do you have in mind?"

"Nothing in particular, yet. Just a nagging thought that unless people can get through the stress enough to move from, what did you call it? Preservation? Toward wanting to actively make things different, our work at creating something innovative might not make a difference. Besides socializing our general direction, which will help us tremendously by the way, what else can be done to move people toward wanting to change?"

"You mean to get them out of their cave?"

"Yes, I guess so. What can be done to help your people be ready to take a risk on something new?"

There was silence on the other end of the phone. Alicia pondered the question for a moment and then, not coming up with an answer herself, she decided to challenge the firm she had hired: "What do you recommend?"

Kate was prepared. "The same thing that I had to do to get my own team working differently—first, emphasize the need for a change in thinking: instead of running from the cause of the stress, run toward it. It's about creating a sense of urgency that will get the change moving forward. Allow people to experience the reality of the situation for themselves and to recognize that they are ultimately responsible for either getting through it or not. They need to understand the consequences of both."

"Consequences of both? What do you mean? Isn't the consequence of getting through it obvious? I mean getting though it means you've succeeded."

"It may seem that way. But there are costs involved with success that people on the team need to be sensitive to, such as the fact that they will have to work hard to get through it. They may need to think differently than they are used to. They may need to recognize and eliminate old ways of thinking. They may need to give up things that they had previously held dear."

"I see. So how did you get your team to recognize the need to think differently?"

"I gave them your feedback full throttle!" They both laughed a little at that, glad they could do so and move on from that point. "I let them feel the dissatisfaction on the part of their client. They needed to feel ownership of that dissatisfaction, so I also got them thinking about how they work together. They needed to realize that they each played a role in the process that led them to a pretty average outcome. Also, I'm a believer that it isn't change that people resist, it's the discomfort that comes along with doing things differently that they resist. So once I created the case for change, that sense of urgency, I began to put in place a process that would guide and support them through change."

Alicia stopped her. "Yeah. I'm not sure how willing my team will be to look at themselves like that."

Realizing that asking her client to be self-reflective was not in the scope of her project, Kate decided to back off from this direction. Her client did not have the same language around the universal creative process to sort through their style differences, so this line of thinking wasn't going to be helpful. Carefully, she tried to redirect her explanation in a way that would be useful to Alicia for getting her team ready to accept new ideas.

"Well, I also helped them have a discussion about new ways of looking at their work. Just talking about what novelty was and the positive potentials that innovation can provide seemed to help them be more comfortable with it. In fact, their energy changed from being frustrated to kind of excited. Now we're down a new path, doing some serious work that, if received well, may just get Consolidated to the next level."

"So you're saying that engaging my colleagues in a discussion about potential paths might loosen them up a bit?" Alicia asked, considering already how she might begin this conversation.

"Yes. That conversation along with the one related to the costs of staying the same can really make a difference."

"I'll see what I can do." Alicia sounded like she was at least entertaining the idea. "I can hardly wait to hear what you are coming up with. I hope it makes all this worthwhile," she added.

"I think the work we're doing will prove its worth to you. You have confirmed the general direction we've taken. Now we have a lot more work to do refining and developing the recommendations before our work is done." Kate paused a moment before pressing on the need for Alicia to take some action with her team. Alicia's commitment to ready her peers was too important to leave it unspecific. "So what are your thoughts about how to have that conversation with your peers?"

"You mean when I tell them that the situation we are finding ourselves in is our own fault?" she asked somewhat sarcastically, then quickly swept her own frustrations under the rug. "No, I know what you mean. I need to be sure they feel the need to do something differently as much as I feel it. I think I know how to do that. We have a monthly leadership meeting next week. I'll put it on the agenda as 'potential strategic directions.' That'll at least get their attention."

As the conversation drew to a close, Alicia was feeling excited to hear the new ideas and began pressing subtly. It took all of Kate's self-control not to give too much of the solutions the team had generated. She wanted to keep Alicia excited and focused on her own job—instilling the need for newness rather than getting into the particulars of the team's plan. They both hung up the phone charged up about new possibilities.

Satisfied that the team was making progress in the right direction, Kate returned to the conference room. On the door, she found a handwritten note to the maintenance group for the building that read, "Please do not clean this room." She entered slowly, wondering what she would find. The room was deserted but the walls of the room were covered with the creative output of the group. She checked the wall clock and realized that it was almost 7:00 PM. Rather than going any deeper into the work of the team by herself, Kate decided it was time to go home. She was sure the team would want to walk her through their work in the morning. Time to rest up, she thought. Tomorrow was going to be a long day—one of many.

chapter 13

The Pieces Come Together

W hen the team regrouped at 9:00 the next morning, each member seemed ready to get to work. The process the day before yielded some promising results, but that didn't quench the team's anxiety and eagerness to hear from Kate about her discussion with Alicia.

"It was a good conversation," Kate began. "Not only did I confirm we are on a very productive path but I also talked with her pretty straightforwardly about how she can help our ideas get heard."

"What do you mean, 'get heard'?" asked Amy.

"Just greasing the rails so that when we present our recommendations, they will be given fair consideration rather than being dismissed offhand."

"Excellent," Juan said, verbalizing the wave of relief that was flooding the room. Now they could move on!

Juan got right down to business. "As you can see, we've been converging on several areas for growing Consolidated's relationship with the market. Before we broke for the day we were able to group the ideas into several general categories, each of which needs additional research and development."

"Yes, I see," said Kate, perusing the work covering the walls of the conference room. From one end to another, sticky notes holding ideas—some of which were very creative, Kate noticed with satisfaction—were grouped in titled categories.

"That wall has over two hundred ideas on it—some of which were totally not worth exploring," Amy said.

"But we didn't dismiss them easily," Damon broke in. "Those babies produced a lot of discussion. Preserving novelty is not easy."

"How did you make sure you did that, preserve novelty?" asked Kate.

"We each had to force ourselves to look at the ideas differently. We asked each other 'What do you like about this idea?'—which at times turned out to be a lot harder to answer than we thought it would!"

Damon was clearly enthusiastic about the process—his smile was buoying up the group's spirits considerably. "Some of the ideas that we initially put in the trash can were reexamined with that "being appreciative" concept in mind and they actually morphed into new, workable ideas, just like you said they could. So we added those to our wall and went on with the grouping."

"Sounds great. Let me ask you all this: if we explored the best ideas here, the best groups of ideas, would we be meeting the mark of providing our client with some real breakthrough results?"

The group didn't hesitate. A confident, collective "yes" came from all five members in unison. Without a doubt, they were clearly committed to the process and invested in its results. Completely independent of her logical side, Kate's heart involuntarily swelled with pride—for them and a little bit for her, too. They were pulling it off. They were becoming an innovative team.

Juan and Amy walked Kate through each of the groupings. Five main themes emerged as essential to building alliances in the marketplace—globalization, technology, supply chain, staffing, and partnerships.

"Kate," Amy finally said after the team talked over the potential directions the ideas could take within each broad theme. "We think it's time to open up the doors here. We need more expertise, more manpower, in order to effectively explore these areas. If we are going to pursue each of these areas with the appropriate amount of attention they deserve, there is a lot of work to do and we can't manage that alone."

"I was expecting we might need some support. Tony has already approved the idea of us pulling some people off other projects to do some more work here. Mostly from the business analyst pool as well as some support staff to help us compile and present our best thinking."

"That's great news. As we discussed next steps at the end of the day yesterday, we were all in agreement that creating subteams to dive deep into these ideas and develop something comprehensive was the best approach," Elaine explained. "The five themes also lend themselves nicely to each of us leading the subteams. Convenient, no?"

"Yes, perfect," Kate added. "Tell me more about your plan."

Elaine took the lead with the pure anticipatory joy of a Golden Retriever faced with a Frisbee. Her tendency toward implementation was finally able to be satisfied. She explained the plan for developing the ideas, including the structures of the subteams, expected outcomes, and aggressive timelines for deliverables. She was clearly in her element. Her voice was enthusiastic and forthright. Juan and Maya seemed to be paying close attention to the content of her plan, following each step as it was presented to be sure nothing was missed. Amy seemed somewhat disengaged, which Kate thought was odd. Damon, however, was beaming. Kate wondered if it was relief that someone else was spearheading this part of the process that made him so happy or something else. Whatever it was, Kate's earlier fear that Damon would disengage during this part of the process seemed unfounded.

When Elaine had finished her thorough layout of the plan, Kate decided to find out. "Damon, I couldn't help but notice you have a happy little grin on your face. Does this plan excite you?"

"To be honest, Kate, I am just glad that Elaine is here," Damon said.

"What?" Elaine said, surprised that Damon was being so openly complimentary.

"This is your part of the process, isn't it? Maybe this is why we occasionally butt heads. I am an ideator and you are clearly an implementer. Just look at how excited you are at finally getting down to business, putting the plan together. I would be dying right now trying to map out all these steps. I mean, I can do it, but I sure wouldn't find any pleasure in it. This stuff makes you glow."

"Yes, this is where I like to spend my time. I love putting together a solid plan and then making it happen. That's why when you're off in Idea Land I try to call you back to Fact World. I want to build something and you're being all . . ." Elaine tried to come up with the right word.

Maya found it for her. "Divergent?"

"Exactly. All that diverging is like floating in the air to me. It needs to come down to earth at some point."

"Right now, I am very glad we have someone who not only likes being where the rubber meets the road, but is also pretty good at it." Damon's compliments were a welcome surprise to the team. Kate was relieved to see Elaine and Damon begin to come together so well, to openly appreciate each other's differences. The shift from when they first started was remarkable. She was convinced that without paying attention to the qualities of the team members and the process they were engaged in this appreciation would never have occurred and their results would certainly have been less significant.

"Me, too," added Amy, as if coming out of a state of hibernation. "The implementation phase is exhausting to me. I'm glad we have someone who is strong in this area."

"That's an interesting question." Juan's mind had wondered away from the interpersonal and back to the theoretical. "Just because you prefer to spend time at one point or another in the breakthrough thinking process, does that necessarily mean you are good at it?"

"What do you think?" asked Amy.

"I think it would make sense if it did, but then again, some of Damon's ideas weren't always the best." Juan smiled at Damon.

"Hey—don't judge, remember?" Damon said.

"I'm kidding a little, but think about it a minute. What if your preference was to come up with ideas and you just weren't all that good at it? Or if you were like Elaine and enjoyed coming up with plans and implementing them but kept missing steps? Do you think that could happen?"

"I think so. I mean preference doesn't necessarily mean skill. You've got to have both to be good at something, I would think," said Amy, intrigued at exploring the idea.

"I don't know about that," Maya spoke up. "I mean, I don't think I have much of a preference at all for one or the other of the stages in this process and I think I can be good at all of them. I don't think you need a clear preference to be good at something."

"That's true," Damon said. "I mean I didn't get to this point in my career without implementing a few things successfully. I love the idea-generation part of the process but if that was all I could do I wouldn't be able to succeed. I don't get turned on by implementing, so I'm seriously grateful that Elaine does, but I have been able to do it when pressed."

"Of course, you must have," Elaine reflected. "I think where people can run into trouble is when they rely too much on their preferences. If all I did was implement, implement, implement, I might implement myself off a cliff. I have to be a clarifier at times so I know in which direction to head."

"Have you ever found yourself leaving the gate too soon?" Juan asked. "I felt you were ready to get going early on in our process. It seemed to me that I was beginning to hold you back."

"Yes, I've done that before. No question about it. Right now I am really glad you did hold us back. Without that mind-mapping thing, we never would have ended up in the direction we have. Exploring the data was key," said Elaine. "And although I can now appreciate that as I look back on our process, I still know that I have no energy to do that work. For me, it's tedious. Next time, I'll use the mind map when I have to do this—that got us out of a rough patch."

Kate was sitting back admiringly watching her team go. What was it that was making this team that was so incompatible at the start work so well together now? It was more than following the breakthrough process. It was something else. Through learning about the process, they had gained an appreciation for each other and their strengths. They understood more about why they behaved the way they did and that understanding was helping them come together around a common goal. Most teams are so busy doing that they are not able to think about their own thinking and manage their own processes objectively. The team had moved quickly to a high level of performing through this understanding of preference and process. She made some notes of her thoughts to bring to Tony later on.

"Kate, you're awful quiet over there. What are you writing?" Damon asked.

"Just a few observations." At first, she wasn't going to share her thoughts with the team for fear of taking them in a direction they didn't need to go. With Damon's direct question, she was on the spot. Instead of being direct about her thoughts, however, she thought it best to test them out.

"I'm wondering, has discovering your preferences for different parts of the process helped this team?" she asked.

Around the table were instant reactions that it had, so she swapped her closed-ended question for an open-ended one. "How has it helped?"

"If I hadn't known that Damon's preference was ideation and that we needed him for that, I would have killed him long ago," Elaine said jokingly, and then added, "but knowing my own preference has helped me more. I mean, I had to actively force myself to do the other parts of the process that I would have preferred to just get through quickly."

"I agree," added Juan, "and the tools we've been using have helped with that. It has been great knowing where we are in the process and where we are going. I like to spend my time clarifying and developing, so when it was time to come up with ideas, I knew to be more patient. It was more important to generate a lot of ideas instead of a few usable ones. Usually, I would stop there. You know, just come up with a few ideas that I found workable and move on. Knowing where we were in the process and having some tools to use to get me to think differently helped me make it through that phase with a little more comfort. You just have to trust the process is going to take you where you need to go."

"What tools are you talking about?" Damon asked.

"Like when Tony came in with those toys. Those were tools of sorts, weren't they?" said Juan.

"Yes," said Kate. "They were tools used for helping people come up with new ideas by relating things to each other that they wouldn't normally try to combine. It's called 'forced connections.'"

"I thought so. That got my mind working differently and the guidelines did, too. I would never have expected something as simple as guidelines would make such a difference."

"Yeah, I've been in lots of meetings before when we would generate ground rules during the first meeting," added Amy, "and then set them aside and hardly ever think about them again. It made for a lot of wasted time in terms of the time generating them and then the time wasted not following them. These guidelines were different, though. We made an effort to really use them and hold each other accountable to them. I've been in brainstorming sessions before where there were no guidelines and that led to a small number of ideas, boring ones at that. I think that was because people would criticize them so much no one would take the risk of putting something new out there."

Wanting to own up to her own insights, Elaine added, "And we used the stages deliberately so that we were all applying our thinking, no matter our preference, to the task at hand. It's just way more efficient to have everyone focused on the same thought process—and for me to realize that I can't rush the process to get to action steps."

"Can I say something here?" Maya said. "I think I'm missing something because I don't know how awareness of preference has really helped me. Like I said before, I don't think I have a preference. I'm pretty comfortable with all the stages of the process."

"So you didn't use that knowledge at all as a part of this team?" Kate challenged her.

"Yes. Yes, you did," Amy said. "It wasn't the same as Elaine and Juan being more aware of themselves. It was more about you being aware of where others were in the process and helping them come together. There were a bunch of times you helped me see the importance of a part of the process I didn't particularly get. For instance, I'm not all that much into implementing plans. I love data so clarifying is comfortable for me. Generating ideas and developing them is great. But I'd prefer to continue to make an idea stronger than let it go. Juan and I have that in common. Last night as we were working on these, we were both getting in tinker mode—you know what I'm talking about? We were sort of adjusting things."

"I like to tinker, it's true." Juan agreed.

"And he and I were spending a lot of time in the globalization group over there. I could tell you were getting a little impatient. You wanted to work with Elaine to come up with a plan of attack and had already started imagining how our subteams might look. Instead of pushing us too hard, you were able to get Juan and me to finish our work more quickly. Instead of just saying, 'That's it—we've got to get on with it.'"

"Like I wanted to say," Elaine interrupted.

"You actually helped him finish." Amy continued, "It was as if you understood that tinkering was something we had to do and it was better to just help him through that phase than to squash it."

"I did? How did I do that?" Maya was surprised.

"I remember this," Juan interrupted. "We were looking at the ideas under globalization and Elaine began talking about moving forward and mentioned a couple of steps that needed to be done. You said something like, 'Yes, we do need to move on,' but instead of trying to stop our work, you asked us a couple of questions that got me to finish what I was doing faster. What did you say again? It was something simple like, 'What are you seeing here?' that started our conversation. In just talking about it, you brought us back to task and helped me concentrate on finishing. And that's when we noticed the staffing issue was embedded in the globalization issue. We pulled that out and made it into a fifth category."

"I think you are what's called an integrator," said Kate. "By not having a distinct preference you can be flexible throughout the whole process; you can also help us move forward when we need to. That's what it sounds like you did here. You went and helped Juan finish up so you all could move ahead. That would be hard to do if you weren't comfortable with all parts of the process."

"I guess I can see that," Maya said. "I hadn't thought about it like that. More often, I don't see my not having a clear preference as an advantage but a liability. It's like I feel pressure to be everything in the process or be good at everything. Sometimes I just want to move on."

"I'm glad you did it," Juan assured her, "but it was the way you did it. You felt comfortable with the process, helped me do what I felt I needed to do, and then we got out of the gate."

Maya was pleased. She had been unsure about how she was contributing. Being comfortable with everything felt to her like she wasn't specialized enough or that she needed to be stronger in more parts of the process. Now she realized that was not the case.

"Not to be too much of the task master that I am," Elaine began, "but we need to finish up here. All this reflective talk is well and good but we have some work to do."

Kate bristled a little bit. "Elaine, we do have work to do and I think you've laid it out very nicely. But I don't want to diminish the value of what we've been talking about here. This reflective time we are having is essential. It's what is making this team outperform other teams and more important outperform itself. You guys have done more work in new and different ways in the last week than you have all year. I'm very proud of you all. We are almost to the finish line and I can see the directions we are taking our client in are right in line with what they need."

"Of course, you're right," Elaine said. "I can't argue with the results. We got here not just by reflecting on how we were doing but trusting that the process would take us there."

"It has so far," Maya interjected, also ready to move along. "What's next?"

chapter 14

What's the POINt?

"**N**o idea is perfect," Kate stated. "We are at that stage where we are going to need to test, measure, and tinker with the ideas and directions we've chosen. I also like the idea of subgroups to tackle each area. But I would like to make sure we are using a common process. We need to be clear about that before we continue with the divide-and-conquer plan."

Elaine was getting antsy. Doing more work to develop the ideas was a draining thought to her. She was ready to get something to the client. In her mind, it had taken a long time to get to where they were and her patience had been tested every step of the way. She thought she had the answer at the beginning and, although it was one of the answers they chose, it wasn't the only one—so she saw the value of completing the process. Somehow that didn't make it any easier to recognize that they were in the developing stage and not yet to implementation. She was ready to get the work done.

Juan and Amy had a different mind-set altogether. They were excited to start seeing what would work and what wouldn't for their client. It was another opportunity to test, measure, and dig into data. It was a chance to refine and perfect. They both wanted to be involved in this part of the process as much as possible and the subgroup idea might not enable that.

Juan spoke up. "Wait a second, guys. I know we talked about subteams as a good method for moving forward, but what if we have a few areas we like to be a part of? What if I'd like to contribute to several groups?"

"Yes, I'm interested in going deep into a couple of these categories," added Amy.

Maya understood their points but recognized that the time had come to move on. "I know how you both feel. And at the same time I think Elaine's point about saving time is also a good one. What if we all get the deep dive done in small teams and then come back together to review each other's work? Then we'd get input into other teams but not be slowed down too much."

Juan had to agree this made sense. He appreciated the urgency of his teammates and knew it was his tendency to want to slow things down. "OK," he said, "I'll still go with that as the plan but I think Kate's right that we will need some consistency in how each of our teams approach their challenge. If each team refines and develops differently, it will be hard to fit it all together in the end."

No one disagreed or added to Juan's remarks, because most were just grateful to be moving forward.

The team looked toward Kate. She was ready. "We got to where we are by trusting the process, let's not lose that now. Developing is the phase we are in, so let me first remind you that this is about looking for ways to strengthen the ideas so that we bring the best ideas to the table in a coordinated and complete manner. It's the time to test our assumptions, measure what we can, and be sure that what we recommend really hits the goal. And what is our goal here?"

"To bring the client some new, workable, creative directions," said Amy.

"That's basically how I understand it," Juan said, supportively.

Kate continued, "In the course of developing, we may find ourselves needing more facts, more understanding of context. What tools do you tend to use to sort out what is good about the ideas and what might require some more thinking?"

"You mean a SWOT analysis?" Amy said immediately. "Listing strengths, weaknesses, opportunities, and threats."

"Sure, that's a pretty standard tool used in many businesses. But let me ask you this: how well does it use the convergent guidelines? In looking at weaknesses and threats, for example, how does it help you preserve the novelty of the ideas? How would SWOT be affirmative?"

"Well, it's not really meant to be a 'breakthrough thinking' tool. I've used it to pick apart an idea and see what I should be concerned about," Amy added.

"And I bet it works great for that," Kate said, "but that's not what we need here. We need a tool that is going to help us take the best part of the idea forward and come up with ways of developing the parts of the idea that might not work as well. What I like to do is called POINt." She wrote the word on the whiteboard vertically with the *P* on the top.

"Its not polite to point," Amy smiled.

"What does it stand for?" asked Juan, oblivious to Amy's playing around.

"Plusses, opportunities, issues, and new thinking. It uses some of the same techniques we have been using in other parts of the breakthrough thinking process, such as phrasing concerns as questions, and incorporates the guidelines of diverging and converging into its steps. Want to give it a try?"

Amy and Juan were most intrigued. Damon, Maya, and Elaine seemed less interested so Kate decided to ask one of them to be her guinea pig. Elaine was always chomping at the bit to get going so Kate asked her, "Elaine, which of the teams do you think you want to lead?"

"Supply chain," Elaine said without hesitation.

"Any else interested in leading that one?"

If anyone had an interest in that area, they kept it to themselves. No one wanted to get between Elaine and her goal. If supply chain was their interest, they would just have to find another one.

"OK, so let's look at some of the ideas in that group. Which one do you immediately think has a lot of potential for getting something new and different for the client?"

"I don't know so much about new and different but I know by looking at the full spectrum that each supplier delivers we might be able to leverage volume to get better deals for Consolidated in the future."

"OK, so is the idea to develop fewer but tighter relationships with vendors?"

"Yes, I think that sums it up pretty well." Elaine felt like Kate was on her side.

"So, group, any questions about this idea?" No one volunteered any so Kate continued, "Then let me ask you, what are some of the plusses of that idea?"

"Stronger alliances with other companies."

"Better costs for products."

"Shorter delivery time."

"Fewer contracts to worry about."

The group continued to diverge for a few more minutes till Kate posed the next question.

"What about opportunities? These are the what-ifs about the idea—the potentials. What might happen if this idea is adopted?" Kate asked.

"We may find opportunities to cross-collaborate."

"We may find more areas to be in business together."

"It might expose Consolidated to takeover."

"What?" said Amy. "I thought we were looking at opportunities?"

"We are, Amy," said Kate, "but are all opportunities positive? This is the 'imagine-if' question that gets us to think like futurists. So we can imagine what might be potentially good or bad. Good question, Amy. Let me remind you all that this is a divergent phase of this tool. Remember those guidelines—defer judgment especially. Now, what other potentials do you see?"

"It might limit their reach into the market."

"It might expose them to risk if a major supplier goes away and they have a lot of contracts to fill."

"It might give them access to the latest new thing before competitors."

"It might link them too closely with their suppliers' financial health."

"It might make them more financially stable to be linked with healthy suppliers."

After a few more minutes of letting the group diverge, Kate said, "I can see there are issues about this idea—things that might need to be addressed before it could actually work. These are the concerns you might have about it. If we were to phrase those issues as questions using the open-ended statement starters we learned before, what would they be?"

"How might we find financially solvent suppliers?"

"How might we be sure we are not too closely linked with any one supplier?"

"How might we take advantage of their new products before our competitors do?"

"How can we be sure we are getting the best products available?"

"How can we be sure we are always getting the best price?"

After a few minutes, Kate had a concern about the concerns. She needed to find the source of the pain, so she asked, "Elaine, there are a lot of issues around the idea of developing a tight relationship with a few vendors. If we are going to make this idea strong and capitalize on those plusses, we have to tackle these issues. For which issue do you think it is imperative we get some new thinking?"

"How to be sure we are getting the best products available?" Elaine said." If we can show Consolidated that tighter relationships give them better deals, that's great, but what about quality control? How will they know they are still getting the best product for their money?"

"Does anyone have any questions about that one?" asked Kate to a group ready to burst out of their chairs. "OK, let me have some ideas."

"Create an automated search for the product prices."

"Have a person dedicated to watching the competition's supplies—what are they ordering, from whom? for how much?"

"For those products that are ordered more than others, do biannual price checks."

"Buy a small business that can supply 100 percent of the product to Consolidated."

"Is there another, smaller country that can provide a better product?"

The group continued to diverge till the flip chart was filled. Then Kate checked in with Elaine.

"OK, Elaine. You have a lot of options here. Are there any that naturally go together?" Kate facilitated Elaine through the converging process till Elaine focused on the idea that Consolidated would need to set up a process to review contracts biannually. She also liked the idea of finding small suppliers that might be cost effective to purchase outright. "That would require a bit more research." Elaine said as she glanced at Juan, knowing that he would be perfect to do that research.

Juan smiled knowingly and mouthed "not this time" toward her.

"What about the other ideas Elaine started out with?" asked Maya. "Are you saying she should do a POINt on each of those ideas?"

"Elaine, do each of them need a POINt?" asked Kate.

"Some of them do, for sure, but others seem pretty straightforward. The team can go right into analysis of the supplier's product catalogs, for instance. No reason to wait there. But now that we've done this one, I might also ask that they look at the supplier's financial stability as well."

"So as far as process with our groups, then," Damon observed, "it might be good to do the POINt for those ideas that seem big or perhaps not as focused before diving into the ones that seem complete or straightforward. Or is that just me wanting to focus on something divergent?"

More than one group member was a little surprised at Damon's self-awareness but maybe not as surprised as they might have been a few weeks ago.

Maya saw his point. "No, I think you're on to something there, Damon. Going deep into the big ideas seemed to help guide the more easy ones. I think I get this. Tackle the bigger, more ambiguous ones and some of the simpler ones get worked out in the process."

The nods from the team made the table look like it was populated with bobble heads. "Cool," said Damon, "so this is the process we'll start out with. Let's go deep! Who wants which topic?"

The group quickly self-organized, dividing the remaining idea groupings among themselves, and set forth as if with shovels in hand ready to mine for gold.

chapter 15

Assisting Acceptance

O ver the next week, the main team got their subteams together to work on developing the idea groupings they felt were key for their client. After using POINt as their main method of analysis, most of the teams found that they required additional information to further flesh out the main ideas. Globalization needed information on international law. Staffing required the demographic information of current Consolidated employees. Supply chain needed more information on current Consolidated suppliers and began looking at redundancies and cost comparisons. All team leaders, having now experienced the breakthrough thinking process, were able to move their teams through it efficiently. The workable ideas within each grouping were analyzed further. Eventually, comprehensive recommendations based on available data (from not just the usual sources—they wouldn't make that mistake again!) coalesced in their final reports. In the process, some ideas were abandoned as unworkable or not timely. Other ideas were expanded on or morphed into new concepts altogether.

The process of developing and reporting on their recommendations spanned the next three weeks, with each miniteam working long hours. Kate would check in with them every day or two. She would alternate dropping by their meeting place and just stopping by the team leader's office. She felt going in person was better than electronic communication at this point. She needed to see the nonverbal behavior of the people working so hard to get this done in order to intuitively understand how things were going. She needed to see the "face" of the team to be able to target her questions well.

Kate had to walk a delicate balance. If she was too present within each group, she would appear as if she were micromanaging. If she was too absent, a group might forget its connection to the whole. She walked this line deftly. She only provided direction when asked. When she felt they were off course, she would ask purposefully open-ended questions to help the subteams consider alternative courses. She also quietly kept her own notes after each encounter to capture where she felt the subgroup was in the process and what else she'd like to see accomplished. From these notes, she noticed a piece that each team had yet to consider but had been on her mind since her last conversation with Tony—how would Consolidated react to the novelty contained in the new report?

She had laid the groundwork for Consolidated being open to their new report through her conversation with Alicia. Still, she thought the teams would need to consider how Consolidated would adapt to the changes they were proposing as part of their implementation plan. They needed to foster acceptance right from the start.

Toward the middle of the third week of developing, she called a team meeting to reconnect with everyone and give them one more tool to foster acceptance.

"Everyone, I have to say I'm very impressed with the work of the subgroups. I can see you're all working hard to finish by the end of the week. Some of your teams are putting together recommendations; others are still supporting recommendations with data. Elaine, I think your group is basically done—on to formatting."

"It's not what you think," Elaine blurted. "We did not leap to solution and implementation. I know you think we did, but supply chain was very straightforward. It was mostly about process improvement and changing a few supplier contracts, adding to some, eliminating some."

"Uh-huh ... ," said Damon. He and Elaine traded less-than-fully-evolved looks at each other.

"It's OK, Elaine. I watched your progress. I saw you keeping everyone on track but your implementation side never took over," Kate said, glancing at Damon. "But because you are all nearing the end with your teams, I wanted to bring you together and ask about how your section might be received. So just let me ask you to consider these two questions," she said as she unveiled a previously covered pair of flip chart papers. Each flip chart had one question written as its headline:

"What might help your client accept your proposal?"

"What might get in the way of their accepting your proposal?"

Doing a very poor impression of Yoda from *Star Wars,* Juan said, "The tool belt is strong in this one, I sense." Juan was making jokes? Juan? Things have changed, they all thought, amazed.

"Yes, it's a pretty easy one," Kate continued unfazed. "It's just a targeted way of thinking through the whole of the implementation. Basically, it addresses something that a lot of organizations either overlook or diminish the importance of in order to get a product out the door. It's how we are going to help Consolidated begin managing change. It's all about overcoming resistance and gaining acceptance."

The face of each team member seemed attentive and ready to see where this was going so Kate plowed ahead.

"First, let's talk for minute about why we need to do this. Why do you think we should start helping Consolidated manage change now rather than waiting till the ideas are accepted and being implemented?" Kate asked.

Maya reacted immediately. "Didn't you already do this when you spoke with Alicia?"

Amy followed, "Yes, wasn't that what your conversations with Alicia have been about?"

"Absolutely," said Kate, "but managing change is a process; it doesn't happen all at once. You can't just check it off your to-do list and say 'there, done.' It takes time to go through a process, and at each step of implementation it's worth checking in with the notion of how we are managing change."

Elaine was intrigued. "When I have implemented things in the past, I can't really say I even paid attention to how people manage change. I mean, they either get on board or they don't. That's their problem. The plan still gets implemented."

"Smoothly?" Juan asked.

"Sometimes yes, sometimes no. But the plan still gets implemented," Elaine continued.

"I can tell you from where I sit that that approach makes me uncomfortable," Juan followed. "I have to know more about a plan before I can implement it. I have to be very comfortable with the whole idea."

"Yes. That's the clarifier in you. I can see that," said Maya. "It's not unreasonable to think that many people might need some time to be on board with a change. And here we are presenting something really new and different. If people are not comfortable with what's being presented initially, why would they follow it through?"

"I've been on teams charged with implementing things where the people we asked to do the heavy lifting would say, 'Yes, sure, let's do it,' and then not do anything," added Juan. "It was as though they didn't like it, didn't feel they could say anything, so they would agree to it and then passively let it fail."

"And whether they get on board with it starts at the beginning," Amy said matter-of-factly. "Have you ever seen anything like that when you implement something, Elaine?"

Elaine thought for a moment. "Yes. I've had that trouble at times." She looked at her laptop in front of her uncomfortably. "I guess I see what you're saying."

"The people we are going to present our work to will be ready for novelty, at least that's what Alicia has led me to believe," said Kate, "but we have to assume there will be some resistance to what we present right off the bat. If we can anticipate that resistance and leverage those things that might enable acceptance, then we stand a chance of succeeding with getting something new in place."

"Is that what this tool is for?" asked Damon.

"Exactly. It gets right to that point quickly and efficiently. It's called 'assisters-resisters' and it's a way of targeting some divergent thinking toward managing change."

The group was silent, focused, and ready to hear more, so Kate continued. "On the first page, as you can see, you identify things that are going to help get the ideas accepted. When it comes to implementation, these are the things we will be sure to leverage."

She continued, "The second page is where you put those things that may get in the way of the idea being accepted. In a minute, I'm going to show you how to use these to produce some action steps that you'll want to incorporate into your proposal."

"So it's a list," Juan said, somewhat disappointed. Secretly he was hoping there'd be more toys involved.

"Yes, but not a free-form list. For this, I'd like you to identify the answers to the questions in five categories. These are the standard categories every newspaper reporter has to gather information in order to put together a story. It's the five Ws. Do you know what those are?"

"Who, what, where, when, and why," Amy said immediately.

"Exactly," said Kate, writing each of these words on the flip chart as she continued to explain. "On this first page, identify who is going to assist your ideas in being accepted. Who will champion them? Then, what kinds of things might help your ideas be accepted? Then look at whether there are places that might be of assistance. After that, are there any times that will help you get the ideas accepted? And last, what are the compelling reasons the ideas should be accepted?"

Amy, Maya, and Juan all began speaking at the same time. "Hold on." "What do mean by 'What are some times that will help?'" "What do you mean by 'places'?"

"Good questions. I think the best way to show you is for you to see the tool in action. Elaine, because your group is farthest along, can we try using this tool on what you've been working on?"

"Sure," she replied.

"Thanks. Would you please give the rest of the group a short synopsis of your report?" Kate asked. "Emphasis on short, please; just give enough information for the team to get a sense of where you and your group are taking our client."

"Well, like I said before, supply chain was a very straightforward area. We mapped out some processes that they were currently using to receive the supplies they need for their products. You know, Consolidated produces a lot of things and we couldn't do everything, so we focused on their main brands, about 80 percent of their profit base. We found that some contracts with the suppliers made no sense; others simply needed to be leveraged more effectively. In one case, we found they were receiving the same materials at different costs from three different suppliers. Why this was never found is beyond me. We also found that some suppliers actually had more completed versions of the product Consolidated was buying and then assembling itself. They are buying aluminum sheets for making their own cans when they could buy the empty cans already assembled at a price only slightly more than the sheets. That change alone should result in an enormous one-time savings in manufacturing costs. So we're making some pretty specific recommendations for changing their business and their relationships with several of their suppliers."

"And this is going to affect the part of their business that produces 80 percent of their profits?" Juan clarified.

"Yes. But it makes so much sense. I honestly cannot see how anyone would be against our recommendations. Really straightforward stuff."

"Perfect. Any other questions for Elaine before we get into it?" Kate asked. There were none. So they began with Kate filling in the flip charts. "Who might help this idea get adopted?"

The answers streamed from the team:

"The head of finance."

"The CEO."

"Alicia."

"Board members."

"Accounting."

"The suppliers, at least some of them."

After a few more minutes of diverging, Kate asked her next question. "What are some things that will help get these ideas accepted?"

"The budget."

"The annual report."

"The focus on profit."

After a few more responses, Kate asked a weirder W question. "Where are some places that will help get these ideas accepted?"

"Not the cannery, that's for sure," Damon laughed.

"OK, so that might be a resister. I'll put that on the other sheet, but let's try to stay focused on the assisters. Where are some places that will help get these ideas accepted?" Kate repeated.

"The board room."

"The break rooms."

"The loading dock."

"See? That wasn't so hard. Let's go on to another one. "When are some times that might help get these ideas accepted?" There was a pause. Kate waited. The pause continued. Kate had an expression that said that she fully expected them to come up with some answers. She was sure someone in the team would bend before she would have to rephrase the question. Finally, Juan spoke up and then others followed.

"Annual report time."

"Yearly stockholders' meeting."

"Day shift."

This one seemed to run out of steam quickly, so she just moved on to the last W question. "Finally, the why. Why will these ideas be accepted?"

"It makes financial sense."

"It would reduce costs."

"And labor."

"It simplifies the process."

"It makes life easier."

After a few more minutes of diverging, the group was clearly satisfied with their exploration and out of more reasons to add. Kate congratulated the group on a job well done and then asked for them to consider the negative side. "Who might resist the new ideas?"

"Can they be some of the same people that were on the assist side?" asked Maya.

"They often are," replied Kate.

"Board members."

"The unions."

"The cannery personnel."

"Some front-line managers."

She continued down her list of resisters till the sheet was almost filled. Some of the potential points of resistance she wrote included the following:

"The trucking union."

"After harvest season."

"Because people may see a lot of hassle in changing."

"Because they have nowhere to store the cans they buy."

"Because they don't think saving money is as important as keeping jobs."

"Now here's the challenging part. Remember how I've asked you to use a couple of stems to form questions? We did that in the clarifying part of the process and again within the issues part of the POINt process. Each one of these resisters is a new issue to be addressed. They are opportunities for a new question. The answers to those questions will be terrific action steps. Let's give it a try." Kate was enthusiastic. She wrote, "How to ... ?" and "In what ways might ... ?" up on the whiteboard of the conference room.

Comfortable with the process, the group went right to work.

"How might we get the unions on board with the changes?"

"How might we protect against job loss and still realize a gain?"

"In what ways might we redeploy or reuse the canning equipment?"

"How might one-on-one conversations about the change be initiated in the break room?"

"How might the board members support the changes?"

"How might we increase ownership of the change?"

"How will the inevitable discomfort that comes with change be dealt with?"

After a few more challenges were named, Kate began to take the team to the next level. "Which of these questions do all of you think is most important for Elaine's group to address in their presentation of recommendations? Let's do the check mark voting again. Take a marker and put a check near the top three questions Elaine's group needs to address."

After the vote, there were three questions with five votes each and one with six.

"How did one end up with six votes?" Juan wondered aloud.

"I voted for it twice. It's that important from my point of view," Damon said with certainty.

"Apparently, everyone agrees. Shall we work on that one?"

"If it's all the same, everyone, I think I'd like to take this back to my team and get them thinking about the answers. There's no need to replicate the same steps here that I'll be doing with my team later today. I get this and I see some issues we didn't address earlier. We're going to have to stop the presses on that report," Elaine said. "And here I thought I wasn't moving too quickly."

"You weren't, Elaine. No team had yet addressed the issue of accepting the changes that new ideas bring. That's why we needed this meeting. I wanted to be sure you each had managing change on your radar and a consistent method of doing it."

"And now we do." Damon smiled that room-swallowing grin of his.

"Good," Kate smiled back, "but let me emphasize one point before we break. The answers to your points of resistance can become action steps in your implementation plan. They may take the form of provocative questions to ask your audience during your report or they may be specific recommendations you can make for implementing your ideas. Just be sure to leverage those assisters in ways that work. You don't want to lose those."

"You've got to play to your strengths," Damon said, making a note.

"Questions? Concerns?" asked Kate. "Ready to get busy?"

The bobble heads responded in the affirmative. "Great! If you have some ideas about any of the points of resistance we were just working on, please give them to Elaine as soon as you can. And could I just add one more thing? Thanks. Thanks for being flexible today and making the time for this meeting. And thanks again for being open to different ways of accomplishing things. I'm looking forward to seeing the final reports come together. What is a reasonable time frame for presenting the final version to Tony?" said Kate.

"Next Friday?" asked Damon.

"Can we make it any sooner? I'm sure he'd like to schedule the meeting with Alicia for before the end of next week." Kate pressured them but knew they would respond well.

"Would Tuesday be all right?" he asked. "Then we'd have another day to make the final changes before showing it to her on Friday?"

"I'd like more editing time. After Tony sees the mountain of stuff before him he's going to ask us to whittle it down. That's one little bit of resistance I see right away," Amy said knowingly.

"So how might we make it more concise right now?" asked Maya, smiling.

"Nice," smiled back Amy at the use of the "how might" question. "I've got to be honest, guys. This is the part of the process that's hardest for me. I'm going to need more time to make sure the report is ready before we present it."

"I know implementing isn't where you like to be, Amy," Maya said, "but we have got to move on. What is going to help you feel ready to let it go?"

"I think this assisters-resisters thing is going to help. I mean, it will certainly make it stronger and I like to build on things."

"I'm with you, Amy," Juan said, "I'm a data guy, not an implementation person. But what helps me is imagining the finish line and knowing I have to get there. Here we know we need to pare down our reports and anticipate how people might react to change. If I focus on that process as developing data, which essentially it is, I'll get it done."

"I can see that, Juan. But I'm tired. Putting plans together just drains my energy." Amy was, perhaps for the first time in this process, truly weary. Kate could see her wilt like a parched flower. The group was steeped in the language around the breakthrough process at this point, so she decided to not step in. She wanted to see how they would sort it out before intervening.

"We've all been through parts of this process we haven't liked doing," Damon said, "with the possible exception of Maya." Maya took this as a compliment. "What helps me is to refocus on the goal and look for the parts in that stage of the process I do enjoy. I mean, I don't have a lot of energy for implementing either but if I can diverge on steps in the plan I can have some fun."

"Sounds like you and Juan both find that part of the process you enjoy and then exploit it," Kate observed.

"I think it's about recognizing where you are and what is really going to be needed," Maya added.

Amy sighed. They were right. There were parts of the planning process that lent themselves to her particular strengths. She needed to focus on those.

"I can also look for some help within my team," she thought out loud. "I have a couple analysts who I've had to pull back from implementing a couple of times as we were working on our section. I'm sure they could help." She looked up, somewhat embarrassed at exposing her weakness, and saw nothing but concerned and supportive teammates. She straightened in her chair; this time she was a flower awakening with the sun. "Sorry, guys. I've got it now. I know how I can get this done. What did we say, by Tuesday next week? I can make that happen."

Trust the process, Kate thought to herself. *Works every time.*

"OK. Tuesday it is. We'll be ready." Damon clapped his hands. "Let's do this!"

chapter 16

Sealing the Deal

E ach team had prepared its portion of the presentation as if it were the most important part of the presentation, yet they flowed together like a well-reasoned plan. Each recommendation had been thoroughly thought through, not just in terms of viability, but also with the criteria of novelty, value to add, and ability to be accepted as their benchmarks. The ideas built on one another to form a full-fledged strategy. The first hurdle was Tony.

Kate wanted to be sure those in the subteams were recognized for their hard work so she coached each member of her team on how to encourage their people's success. Each subteam member was responsible for the presentation while the team leader listened on, occasionally asking a clarifying question to be sure the information was presented fully. Each presentation had to be succinct yet thorough. They had to present their ideas, the benefits, as well as the potential sticking points. Each had to be compelling and had to anticipate potential points of resistance realistically. They had to find those points of resistance and present workable solutions even before the resistance had been expressed.

For each team leader, this represented a challenge in that they had to have a competent and convincing presenter from their team. Also the material the presenter brought to bear had to be well reasoned and sensible. Their recommendations had to be novel and wise, two things that occasionally are difficult to find in the same place. The team leaders had to spend a few hours with each presenter to be sure that they were competent and well versed in the ideas they were promoting and ready for potential questions. Damon thought it was a lot like the way a candidate might prepare for a town hall meeting. He would try to poke holes in his presenter's arguments, just to try to uncover additional points of resistance. The presenters followed the politico's special formula: know your talking points, listen actively, and seek commonality of purpose—these were the elements of success.

The teams prepared quickly and soon the day had come to present to Tony prior to the big meeting with Alicia and Consolidated. Tony sat back and listened to each presentation over the course of three hours. The leadership potential among the subteam members who presented pleased him greatly. He saw budding talent that he was sure would be relied on over the next several years as more seasoned members of the firm retired. It was these types of experiences that would develop the best successors. As he listened to the presentation he made a note to be more deliberate in developing the high-potential members of the organization. If these types of opportunities were standard practice, the firm would be setting itself up for success in the long run by creating a thick pool of talent to take over when the old guard, like him, finally retired.

Another thing he noticed was that each team member seemed entirely focused on resolving the issue for the client. Posturing for one's own benefit seemed absent from the presentations. He wondered if this was a happy coincidence or if each team had talked about what would make them a success beforehand. In an industry where certainty of expertise was the norm, he found it strangely comforting to see his people seemingly devoid of self-promotion. They let their work speak for itself.

There were a few exceptions to this rule, however. Lyndon Mainland from Elaine's group did seem to overemphasize the ease with which the idea could be implemented. Chris Allen from Juan's group seemed to spend more time than necessary enamored with the reasons for the recommendations rather than the recommendations themselves. And Eleanor Biddle from Damon's group was clearly determined to present as many ideas as possible.

Tony noticed these examples seemed to reflect the style bias of that subgroup's leader. It was continually fascinating to him how styles manifest themselves. He made a note to recommend to Kate that her subteam leaders should edit their presentation for style bias before the final presentation to Alicia and the other senior leadership of Consolidated. If the emphasis remained on the ideas, their client had a good chance of being blown away. He was very happy with the outcomes and was confident their client would be as well.

The day to deliver the end product approached quickly. The team—confident, prepared, and a little anxious—met in the lobby of Consolidated's corporate headquarters prior to the presentation. They stood in a circle, materials in hand, and held a quick powwow.

"We have an hour," Kate reminded them. "They will have a chance to read the report thoroughly after we leave, so we have to be clear with the key points. What's our main goal again?"

"To open their minds to possibilities," Elaine and Amy said almost simultaneously.

"To get them excited about the directions we took," Damon added.

"To make them want to read this tome," Juan added, tired of holding a bag of fifteen 150-page reports.

"And how are we going to do that?" asked Kate.

"We're going to present the data that drove our solutions." Juan was getting ready with his part.

"We are to present the ideas enthusiastically." Damon was also ready.

"We're going to show how these ideas are fully developed," added Amy.

"We are going to show them the bullet points that can guide their implementation." Elaine loved the ending.

"It's all about the results they want. If they want to do something about the data we present, we've got a way forward that hits several fronts at once." Maya was the closer and she was ready to bring it home. "We can help them deliver better products for their customers more effectively."

"Let's do this!" Damon's smile, as always, was infectious. The team was confident and headed into the meeting filled with positive energy about what they were going to present.

■ ■ ■

Within six months of implementing much of the team's recommendations, Consolidated began to show a return on its investment in strategy. Its innovative approaches were being noticed and attempted to be copied by their competitors. Within fifteen months, Consolidated produced record cost savings, increased employee satisfaction, and was able to quantify a higher level of customer loyalty than it had seen in decades. Along with Consolidated, the market itself began to change, with new alliances and crosspollination of ideas forming among the players in the industry almost on a daily basis.

With Consolidated's success, the firm itself saw a resurgence of interested clients. The team members became the core leaders facilitating the breakthrough thinking process with engagement teams throughout the firm. Along with the process itself, the team members taught and spread the principle Kate would so often go back to—success is about knowing yourself and knowing your process. Being aware of how you manage yourself through the process and how you engage with others on your team is central to getting truly innovative results.

Epilogue: Where Are They Now?

Tony Martin

Tony retired from his partner position in the firm. He now is teaching creative thinking in an after-school program at his grandchildren's elementary school. He gets to play with a lot of toys.

Juan Esteban Alvarez

Juan is now a partner at the firm. He is working on creating new algorithms for industry analysis to discover new connections between players in a particular field. His office is consistently covered with very busy-looking flip charts.

Damon Miller

A few years after his experience on the team, Damon left his job at the firm to become a travel writer. Whether it's eating fried grasshoppers in Thailand or making goat's milk ice cream in Ireland, he's known for trying the most unusual things each city he visits has to offer. His *Extreme Travel* show on the Discovery Channel premieres this fall.

Maya Russo

Maya is a very successful team leader within the firm, and is known for her even-handed approach. Her specialty has been entering teams that may not be functioning well and serving as a mediating yet task-driven influence.

Elaine Cassidy

The year after participating on the team, Elaine retired happily to her family's farm in Montana, where she sees immediate results of her hard work. She breeds alpacas and bison to produce yarn that sells for up to $25 per ounce.

Amy Satori

Amy was promoted to partner and is known for being a highly capable innovator who knows how to get ideas to a higher level. When a team finds itself stuck in an early part of the process, they come to Amy. She has the phone at Elaine's ranch on speed-dial for when it's time to implement a plan.

Kate Murdock

After leading the breakthrough team, Kate was presented with many opportunities. Eventually, she chose to join a high-profile consulting firm in Chicago that specializes in creativity and breakthrough thinking. She loves her job.

part 2

Exploring the Four Creative Thinking Styles

chapter 17

Applying the Framework

W henever there is a change in the economy, experts point to innovation as the answer. They will say things such as, "Innovation will drive the new economy." And "we can innovate ourselves out of these problems." To which you might wonder, "Okay, what does that mean? What exactly do I have to do?" This section strives to help you answer that for yourself.

Kate's team gives us an example of how a team that is aware of its process can successfully crack the toughest problems by being intentionally focused on innovation. If you are reading this book, you are likely looking for new ways to solve problems. Whether you are a CEO, team leader, or a team member hardly matters. You have the power to guide innovation no matter what your position is in the organization.

Just as Kate's team discovered, understanding how to deliberately take control of and apply the universal creative process is the first step. The next is to learn how to spot your own and others' preferences within that process in order to set each other up for doing your best (individually and as a team). To innovate successfully you'll need to enhance your team's strengths to their fullest extent—and that's what this section is all about. We'll dive deeper into the FourSight framework, highlighting practical techniques you can apply and customize to your needs. With practice, you'll be able to spot, for instance, an implementer across the conference table before the coffee gets cold and the best donuts are gone. Thanks to that perspective, you'll know what to expect from that person and how you might react in order to keep him or her engaged throughout all of the team's activities. Instead of dreading your differences, you will discover ways of appreciating and strategically using them to your team's advantage. The result will be that rather than ignoring, combating, and blocking each other, your team will find ways to work more efficiently, with less strife, and with targeted results.

chapter 18

Clarifying the Situation

T his is the entry point—the starting gate in any innovation, performance improvement, or problem-solving process. When you clarify, you sort out the real problem from the symptoms or distractions. You look at all relevant data. You measure all aspects of the situation. You ask probing questions. You work to understand the history of the situation and assemble as complete a picture as possible so that you are poised to address the most crucial issues or seize the most significant opportunities. This is your chance to identify that portion of the situation that will have the greatest impact if it is improved. If you succeed, your team's purpose will be clear. If you don't, you may end up solving the wrong problem or moving ahead without enough data to support ongoing decisions.

Innovation is not all about coming up with new ideas. It begins here—figuring out which challenges are the most important and focusing your energies there. Far too often teams do not spend the time clearly examining the situation and defining the challenges. Without this investment of time to clarify, improvement efforts become like shooting in the dark. It is a scattered, inefficient, and ultimately wasteful approach. If we understand the situation well and appreciate the inherent challenges, we can target responses and gain traction from the very beginning.

Innovation is about changing things for the better. Here you know something is amiss so you begin the process figuring out what exactly is wrong. It's kind of like going to the doctor. You know something is not right; you don't feel well, so you seek medical advice. Your doctor cannot immediately prescribe a treatment without first conducting an exam and making a diagnosis—to do otherwise would be malpractice. Essentially, that is what is happening in the clarifying stage. We know we have something to take care of, a predicament (fixing something that's broken) or opportunity (making the most of a good situation). The diagnosis the team makes of the situation is what determines the focus for the remainder of the process. Choose the wrong focus up front and everything else becomes an academic exercise. Choose wisely and the tumblers to the innovation safe align and unlock.

As with every stage of the creative process, there is opportunity to use divergent and convergent thinking.

Challenging yourself to think of new and intriguing data or identify unexplored causes of the issue is where divergent thinking plays a role. Some good questions to ask during this phase include the following:

- What is the history behind this situation?

- What has already been done and what has happened?

- Who is involved?

- Why is this important?

- What is the ultimate goal or desired end?

- What has yet to be explored?

- What else might be going on here?

- Where else might we find relevant information?

- What other data might be useful to know?

- What would each stakeholder in this situation see? What might be their perspective?

Once you feel you have a sense of the overall challenge, it's time to apply some creative thinking as you enter the convergent phase. Here you select the data that is most relevant and most essential to understanding the challenge at hand. The creative opportunity here is to consider unique and unusual information—factors or data that may not have been previously explored. Some questions to ask yourself when selecting important data include these:

- Where else have I seen this before?

- Are there common themes here?

- What stands out as particularly important? Unusual? Intriguing?

- What data give us the greatest insight into the situation at hand?

- What information have we not considered before?

Once you have completed this phase you should have a strong sense of the direction your problem solving needs to take. Ideally, you will have one or two open-ended questions on which to focus your efforts. In our story, Kate and Juan were able to diverge on data and with the team's help find several specific areas to explore. From there, they narrowed their focus on two areas in particular that were new—end-user needs and marketplace compatibility. But this wasn't the end of their work in this phase.

Their next task was to turn these areas of data, these buckets of related information, into challenge questions. They used stems such as "How to . . ." and "In what ways might . . ." to generate a series of challenge questions that invited solutions. Then they converged by selected the ones that seemed to yield the most potential for creative results and moved on to generating solutions to them.

Recognizing Your Team's Strengths and Weaknesses

In the story, Juan was the embodiment of someone with a clarifying preference. He needed time to explore the situation. He became absorbed in the data and saw its value. He was uncomfortable if he felt pushed to move forward too quickly. You can recognize people like Juan on your team because they will likely show the following traits:

- Focus on the task at hand

- Be methodical

- Be organized

- Ask lots of questions

- Be a critical thinker

- Look at areas that have yet to be explored

- Have a high need for information to feel comfortable with the project

- Focus on the details

- Be reluctant to move on to the next step

- Point out lots of obstacles

- Overload teammates with information

Not everyone likes to clarify. Some people, such as Damon or Elaine, have a negative reaction to this step. You can recognize people with a low preference for clarifying because they may do the following:

- Treat data collection in a superficial manner

- Lose patience with detail-oriented research

- Try to move the group into problem solving or action planning too quickly

- Become overwhelmed by too much information

- Become easily annoyed by those who ask a lot of questions

How to Move the Group Through This Stage

Clarifying is all about exploring the situation at hand by asking questions and gathering enough data to steep the team in a deep understanding of the situation. The team will show they have a solid grasp of the situation by creating a few open-ended challenge questions that target core issues. With these questions in hand, the team can move on to the next stage in the breakthrough thinking process.

Knowing the steps in a process and managing people within a process are two different—yet linked—challenges. Steering a group with varied preferences can be tricky, to say the least.

In our story, Kate's challenge was that her team had one strong clarifier—Juan—who seemed cemented into this phase. He couldn't let it go. He needed more and more information to feel he had a clear picture of the problem. Elaine and Damon, however, clearly lacked the interest or patience to work through the data. So to move things along, Kate used two simple techniques: one to help visualize the data and another to frame the right challenge to tackle.

To help understand and sort the data related to their client, Kate introduced the team to mind mapping. This divergent tool is great for identifying relationships with any assortment of information. The team here used it to get a big-picture understanding of all the factors their client was facing in their marketplace. From this big picture, they could zero in on those areas of the map that held the most promise for valuable and novel outcomes—innovative thinking.

Another technique the innovative team used pays specific attention to the fact that how we use language has a direct impact on our thinking. Before the team could move on from the clarifying stage, they had to find a way to focus on their challenge. To do this they used a technique specifically designed to produce the opportunity for great solutions by transforming potential barriers into open-ended questions that invite solutions—challenge questions. Closed-ended or negative statements are a conversational dead end—the pronouncements seem final, like staring at a wall with no clear way around it. Nonjudgmental, open-ended questions focused on the specific challenges at hand, by contrast, and invite solutions and participation. When we phrase a question openly and target it at the challenge we need to face, it invites new thinking and multiple responses.

For instance, in our story the team knew it had to approach the area they described as "market compatibility." If Kate had just said, "Folks, we need some ideas on how to tackle market compatibility. What do you have?" the team would likely have sat there, staring blankly at their leader, their brains mired in the muck of the marketplace. Finding an innovative solution from this statement would be highly unlikely.

Instead, they explored different ways of framing the challenge so they could find other avenues for approaching the problem. They diverged on a few challenge questions such as, "In what ways might we reduce competition?" "How can we work effectively with other businesses?" and "How might we target new markets?" Instead of just stating the topic and asking for ideas, ask for questions that challenge the team to explore where the new opportunities might be. The conscious use of language can make all the difference by enabling the exploration of possibilities.

When moving a team through a process, it is always helpful to have a tool or structure to keep the team on task and engaged. The trick is to use the structure of the team meeting to get the results you need—this is when you need some thoughtful planning and design of your time together. Knowing where you are in the process and what needs to be the outcome of that step is key to getting results.

So how do you move a group through this stage?

- Know the preferences of your team. How might you predict they will behave in this stage of the process? Will they stay in it too long or not long enough?

- Know your own preference so you can manage yourself well during the process.

- Look at the situation from as many varied perspectives as you can to uncover more data.

- Be prepared to use some data-generating questions or a tool like mind mapping to help the team gain a clear holistic view of the challenge.

- When converging, consider which directions are more likely to yield innovative solutions. Which directions were previously unexplored? Which are you excited about exploring?

- Phrase challenges as open-ended questions. Use the stems, "How to ...," "In what ways might ...," "How might ..." to help you create a challenge question that invites solutions.

chapter 19

Generating Ideas

A t some point, the clarifying ends and you need some ideas that will tackle those challenge(s) you've identified. This is the stage where we are seeking that moment of illumination—the "Eureka!" moment. It's the lightbulb going off over your head with the breakthrough needed to resolve the problem. Sometimes this stage proves elusive. Sometimes it happens quickly, seemingly without thinking. With a team, it often happens while brainstorming or using other divergent thinking methods. Like every other step in a performance-improvement or problem-solving process, some people like it and some do not, but it's indispensable. We have to come up with new ideas to improve our approach. Some ideas are radical, producing great change, and others are not so dramatic, producing incremental change. As with all stages in the breakthrough process there is a balance between divergent thinking—a search for many original options, and convergent thinking—the selection of those ideas that hold the greatest promise. In our experience the greatest mistake teams make is the simultaneous application of these two ways of thinking when attempting to come up with ideas. This is akin to trying to drive a car while someone keeps applying the brake—it's inefficient and frustrating.

Diverging

The name of this stage almost implies that it is all about divergent thinking. It's not. Just coming up with a ton of ideas is great but without thoughtful selection the exercise is incomplete. During the divergent phase the focus is on generating as many ideas as possible—essentially answers to your challenge questions—and then selecting carefully the ideas with the most potential for achieving innovative results.

What typically happens is that people will generate a number of new ideas quickly—say within ten minutes. Then, the well seems to run dry and the flow of new ideas runs down to a trickle. At this point, it might be helpful to ask yourself a few questions to spark new avenues of thought. Its been our experience that many groups stop their idea generation before they get to the truly novel ideas, settling only for the first set of ideas that come to mind. As Tony demonstrated in the story, some extended effort can lead to the most original ideas. To stretch your thinking further, take a look at the ideas you've already come up with and ask these questions:

- What can we substitute in these ideas to make something new?

- What ideas can be combined?

- What can we modify about these ideas?

- How can we simplify these ideas?

- How else could these ideas be used?

Remember, the goal of this stage is to force yourself to go beyond the initial brain dump of ideas and open doors to alternate ways of approaching the problem you are working on. Brainstorming is typically how we do this in groups, but think for a minute how you come up with ideas on your own. When do you get those moments of "illumination"? Are you in the shower? Driving? In the middle of a workout?

Sometimes the best approach to finding new ideas is to get as far away from the problem as you can. Once you have a solid understanding of the challenge and you've immersed yourself in the data, step away. Let that information bounce around your subconscious for a while. This is called "incubation." Trust your subconscious mind to do the processing for you and the chances are that when you least expect it, the lightbulb over your head will turn on and a new direction will be clear.

Of course, this doesn't always happen. Sometimes our subconscious is just as flummoxed as our conscious mind. Here's when you can be more intentional about tapping your imagination. Let's say you've been working on a problem for a few days and your brain is swimming in information. You take a break from it and go to the beach. No ideas come to you. You feel your subconscious is falling down on the job. Don't despair. Instead, think about what you experienced while you were away from the problem. What was at the beach? How did you feel there?

Now ask yourself how these experiences might relate to the problem you are working on. Try it. You're guaranteed to come up with a few more innovative ideas that you would not have entertained otherwise.

Converging

Once you think you've got enough ideas to choose from, it's time to decide which ones are worth pursuing—to converge. It might help to group like ideas together—look for themes of ideas. Perhaps there is a family of ideas that speaks loudest to you or maybe you have several distinct directions from which to choose. If you do not have that one clear idea you are ready to develop, then try to pick a general direction—one theme or set of ideas that you feel has the most potential to get you a new and effective result. From looking within that theme, you may try to combine some ideas or come up with one that captures the theme really well.

Recognizing Your Team's Strengths and Weaknesses

In the story, Damon was the ideator extraordinaire. He prided himself on his ability to generate many ideas and was hard to slow down. He was always the first out of the gate with a host of ideas when they were at any stage in the process that called for the group to be coming up with options. You can recognize people like Damon on your team because they will likely show the following traits:

- Like to look at the big picture

- Enjoy toying with ideas and possibilities

- Like to stretch their imagination and often produce novel concepts

- Seem to wander off topic

- Sometimes take a more intuitive approach to things—sharing ideas that make sense to them, but may not be easy for others to follow

- Enjoy thinking in more global and abstract terms

- May overlook the details

- Have fluidity of thought, a seemingly endless production of new ideas

- Overwhelm others with their ideas

- Are not able to stick to one idea

- Are impatient when others don't get their ideas

Other people, such as Elaine or Juan for instance, may show a lack of patience for this stage. Juan was fine with coming up with one or two workable options and felt no need to spend additional time generating ideas when he had what he felt was enough to move on. Elaine would have preferred to get a particular idea and go with it. You can recognize people who may not have a preference for ideation on your team because they may exhibit the following behavior:

- Be fairly quiet

- Be slow to get the ideas flowing

- Offer stable, tried-and-true ideas

- Seem practical and efficient

- Resist original ideas and novel approaches to tasks

- Become fixed on one option without considering alternatives

How to Move the Group Through This Stage

Most people have been through a brainstorming session at one point or another in their lifetime or at least they think they have. Most people think of brainstorming as just getting a group of people together to start generating ideas. It should be noted, however, that idea generation within groups is not necessarily the same thing as true brainstorming. True brainstorming involves a trained facilitator who reinforces the guidelines of brainstorming during the idea generation phase. Research has shown that with a trained facilitator, brainstorming can help produce up to two and a half times as many ideas (both good and bad) as a group working without one. Without that facilitator holding people to the guidelines, these sessions of brainstorming can become idea-killing sessions, rarely producing the desired results.[1]

Ideas may come easy to some and not to others. Some people are comfortable with coming up with lots and lots of ideas and others would prefer to generate just one that works and then move on. Moving through this stage too quickly often produces lackluster ideas and rarely creates a true breakthrough. Stay in this stage too long and you risk overwhelming your people with too many options and nothing gets put into action. Managing your group in this stage is key to achieving breakthrough results.

In our story, Damon's preference for ideating was so strong that others in the group often became annoyed with him. Elaine, however, did not enjoy generating ideas at all—to her, it was a waste of time. Kate was confronted with the interesting challenge of managing team members with completely opposite preferences—a situation that surely happens to most leaders. Also, Kate herself had a preference for idea generation, so she had to first manage herself and not get too enamored with the part of the process she enjoys most by being aware of when the team truly had enough ideas to work from. So what did she do?

The first thing she did was to set ground rules or guidelines for her team to follow as they began to diverge. Kate didn't stop there, however. She also paid attention to the convergent part of brainstorming—the selection of the ideas. She brought out some guidelines here as well to help her team be deliberately more creative.

As a reminder, the divergent guidelines to use with your group when brainstorming are as follows:

- Defer judgment

- Get as many ideas as you can

- Allow for novel thinking

- Look for combinations

The convergent guidelines for preserving creativity while selecting which idea(s) to run with are as follows:

- Be appreciative

- Be deliberate

- Remind yourselves of the goal

- Consider novelty

Thanks to Tony dropping in on their meeting, the team also ended up using a divergent thinking tool called "forced connections." This is a great tool for getting those who may not prefer to be generating ideas involved in the process. It's also a great way to stretch everyone's thinking and get some pretty novel ideas. If you find yourself stuck, or if your team seems to be cooling off too early, you might try pulling out a toy or another object unrelated to the situation you are dealing with and seeing what happens.

In effect, forced connections is a way of engaging your brain in a similar fashion as the beach example used earlier in this chapter. You are taking your mind off the actual problem for a few minutes, thinking about something completely unrelated (toys tend to be good for this), and then going back to the problem at hand. These kinds of brain games, or divergent tools, are great if the facilitator is well versed in their use. Know the game well before you start playing it and you're more likely to have success.

So how do you move a group through this stage of the creative process?

- Know the preferences of your team. How might you predict they will behave in this phase of the process? Will they stay in it too long or not long enough?

- Know your own preference so you can manage yourself well during the process.

- Present and enforce the guidelines for divergent and convergent thinking.

- Be prepared to use some idea-spurring questions or a tool such as forced connections to help the team move on from the obvious ideas and stretch their thinking.

- When converging, look for that sparkling new idea or a theme or general direction to develop into a workable solution.

Note

1. Puccio, G. J., Mance, M., & Murdock, M. C. (2011). *Creative leadership: Skills that drive change* (2nd ed.). San Diego: Sage.

chapter 20

Developing Solutions

Many people confuse creativity with idea generation. That is, they believe that all you need to be creative is to have a novel idea. True creativity brings novelty and usefulness together. A novel idea that has no value is a fad; it will have a very short shelf life. An idea that is original and useful is a true creative breakthrough.

In the idea generation stage we intentionally search for novel ideas; in the developing stage we transform these novel ideas into workable solutions. At this point in the process, you have an idea you think will lead toward a new, potentially innovative solution. Resist the impulse to believe the idea is perfect right out of the box. Sure, it's shiny, new, and very appealing, but no idea is born perfect. It will need some refinement in order for it to be successful. That's what the developing stage is all about—tinkering, adjusting, polishing that novel solution into one that can be implemented successfully.

Have you ever moved too quickly from concept to implementation only to discover in the midst of execution that the idea had some shortcomings? You probably have heard the old saying, "The worst time to build an airplane is when you are flying in it." The time spent on critical thinking in the developing stage helps avoid future problems—such as crashing. The developing stage serves as a test run for the proposed solution. Ultimately you are saving time by ensuring your solution fits your problem.

In all quality improvement processes there is a step dedicated to verifying whether or not the solution you came up with will actually work. It's where you test the new approach and break it if possible. You test the idea, measure its effect, figure out how it might be improved. When you are developing a solution, you want to identify the errors, tinker with improvements, and test, test, test. You are working on improving what you are doing, methodically picking apart and reconstituting those ideas that you thought held the most promise. This is the time to create the best solution you possibly can.

To help strengthen your shiny new idea, consider these questions:

- What are the strengths of this idea?

- What advantages come along with this tentative solution?

- If you implemented this solution, what good things might happen?

- What spin-off ideas might result from implementing this idea?

- What are the drawbacks or limitations of this idea?

- What issues will limit the effectiveness of this solution?

- Looking at the drawbacks and limitations, which ones present the biggest obstacles? How might you deal with these so that they won't stand in the way of success? What might need to change in the idea so these drawbacks or limitations are addressed?

Recognizing Your Team's Strengths and Weaknesses

In our story, the strong developing traits were present in several characters and noticeably lacking in others. Damon, for instance, wanted to check his e-mail rather than develop one of his many fabulous ideas. Juan and Amy were very strong developers, with Amy even saying she loved to improve an idea rather than let it go. That is the strength of developers—they will come up with some near-perfect, well-thought-out solutions. The problem is that perfection takes time and they may never know when to say "this is good enough."

You will recognize the developers in your group, as they will be

- Focused and determined to improve a concept or idea

- Poking holes in weak ideas (often being too nit-picky)

- Spontaneously seeing the shortcomings within an idea

- Highly structured and pragmatic

- Potentially locked into one approach

- Using analysis to refine an idea into a workable solution

- Elaborating and expanding a concept deeply

- Perfectionists

Of course, you are bound to have people like Damon who have an aversion to the developing stage. They will want to move the group along too quickly or they might stop helping entirely. You can recognize those without a preference for developing as they will often do the following:

- Present new ideas rather than work on the ones in front of them

- Unintentionally derail the process by not focusing on the task at hand

- Be focused on action steps and implementation rather than improving the idea on the table

- Be overwhelmed by the scrutiny required to improve on an idea

- Fall deeply in love with an idea and fail to see its blemishes

How to Move the Group Through This Stage

Ultimately, developing is about the team itself. Major innovations tend to happen through group effort. If you asked the question, "Who invented the Space Shuttle?" you'd find the answer is not a single person but a team working together, testing ideas, fitting pieces together. In our story, when it came time to develop different aspects of the report, the team formed subteams that brought in expertise from around their firm. Each team was charged with building out its aspect of the recommendations for Consolidated.

For successful implementation, involving others in the development process is a key part of managing the change. Such involvement not only provides you the skill sets needed to improve your idea, but also increases the sense of ownership of the solution. With that buy-in and increased expertise, your innovative solution stands more of chance of succeeding.

Developing is all about incrementally improving ideas, making them stronger, more targeted, and ultimately more usable. People who prefer this stage will identify appropriate measures, test the ideas, and blissfully try to create perfection. Those on your team without such a preference may lose some energy here. Implementers may want to rush to the end. Ideators may want to still come up with new ideas rather than work to improve the ideas they have already generated. Clarifiers may be continually asking whether the ideas really get at the original question they are trying to solve.

If you are leading a group through this stage, your challenge is going to be to keep the group together and on track. This will likely require a bit of project management skills in assigning appropriate work deliberately, such as measurement or testing activities. Be sure people know where they are in the process and what is coming next so that they don't feel lost.

A tool that's helpful in providing direction for testing and thinking through the qualities is POINt, which stands for pluses, opportunities, issues, and new thinking. In our story, Kate introduced the team to POINt as an alternative to the more commonly used SWOT (strengths, weaknesses, opportunities, and threats), which many organizations use in the strategic planning process. SWOT can be helpful within certain contexts to bring a critical eye to the potential direction an organization might take. But if you are looking to maintain the creative elements of the idea, POINt is more effective in that it doesn't just identify what might not work about the idea or "threats" to it. Instead, it turns those concerns into questions that invite responses that may transform a good idea into a great solution.

Rather than stating a "weakness" such as, "It will cost a lot to get this idea off the ground," which sits there like a black eye on the idea being examined, POINt has you phrase your concern as a question: "How might we reduce the cost of implementing this idea?" or "How might we justify the cost of this idea?" This can open the door to options for development that might not emerge using SWOT. In research conducted with managers who have gone through training in creativity tools and processes, the POINt tool is one of the most-often cited methods used after this training.[1] It is a flexible tool that can be used for more than just evaluating proposed ideas. You can also use it to capture lessons learned from a project, conduct performance reviews, build a business case for a concept, and even provide feedback to someone who has just been observed carrying out a task.

Organizations that are consistently innovative have leaders who know how to help their people think creatively. One of the traits of an innovative leader is the ability to use POINt in the moment with an employee who has a new idea. First, the leader recognizes a new idea being suggested and reacts to the idea with "Here's what I like about that . . ." Then, the leader might follow that with a statement that focuses on the future by saying something like, "If we pursue this idea it might . . . ," sighting a positive potential outcome or future effect of the idea. And to address the leader's concerns about the idea, you might hear the leader say, "I'm concerned about how that might be received by the marketing department. How might you get buy-in for that idea before we implement it?"

The leaders who do this have learned by practicing it. As an experiment you can just try it yourself. We all know what it feels like to get an idea shot down instantly and what it does to our confidence. So the next time you catch yourself reacting negatively to someone's new idea, whether it's from a family member or a colleague, try purposefully starting your reaction with "Here's what I like about that . . ." and go from there. Just be sure you phrase any concerns you have by using a nice open-ended question such as, "How might . . ."

Put yourself on the receiving end of this experiment. If you pitched an idea and got such a question lobbed back at you, what might you do? That's right—you'd develop that idea even more to address that question. You might even appreciate the respectful, interactive reaction so much that you would return to that person again with more ideas. That's the kind of climate an innovative team needs to maintain its imagination and energy. It creates openness to new ideas. Go ahead and practice it at work or home—you'll see immediate results.

So how do you move a group through this stage?

- Know the preferences of your team. How might you predict they will behave in this stage of the process? Will they stay in it too long or not long enough?

- Know your own preference so you can manage yourself well during this stage.

- Use POINt to help critically and creatively examine the solution.

- Involve others so that you have more diversity of thought while increasing the likelihood of early adoption of the solution.

- Use solid project management methods to keep people on track, target test the idea, and begin the change management process.

Note

1. Puccio, G. J., Firestien, R. L., Coyle, C., & Masucci, C. (2006). A review of the effectiveness of Creative Problem Solving training: A focus on workplace issues. *Creativity and Innovation Management*, *15*, 19–33. Firestien, R. L. (1996). *Leading on the creative edge: Gaining competitive advantage through the power of creative problem solving.* Colorado Springs: Pinon Press. Puccio, G. J., & Schwagler, N. (2011, January). *Impact and transfer of creative leadership training within a multi-national corporation.* An unpublished and proprietary research report.

chapter 21

Implementing Plans

S o you've got a creative idea that you are ready to "go live" with—that's what the implementing phase is all about. This is the stage where project plans are created and completed. It's where the rubber meets the road, where the reality sets in, where you are looking for how to make your idea a success. Success is dependent on how well you create and execute your project plan.

This stage is all about action and in many ways about managing change. Those people who are successful at implementing are so because they plan for the best while preparing for the worst. They build steps into their action plans that anticipate potential resistance to the change they are implementing. People who prefer this stage of the process tend to be drivers, known for making quick decisions and getting results. Those who are successful temper this preference with patience and sensitivity to others.

As you think about your plan for implementation of your fabulous new idea, you might want to incorporate your answers to these questions:

- Who needs to be involved? When?

- Who needs to be given the heads-up before the plan is implemented?

- What communications need to be drafted?

- How might the customers view this product? What can be done to shape their perspective?

- What else is happening that may help or hinder the success of this plan?

- What times might be best for implementing the plan?

- Are the reasons for the change clearly laid out?

Recognizing Your Team's Strengths and Weaknesses

Elaine was clearly the strong implementer in our story. Determined and efficient, she was ready to drive home whatever idea was ready to go. She was bottom-line driven and took no prisoners in getting there. You can recognize people like Elaine with a strong comfort with implementation as they are

- Persistent and determined

- Decisive

- Assertive

- Action oriented

When this preference is taken to the extreme, implementers can come across as

- Being too pushy

- Expressing frustration readily when others do not move quickly enough for their liking

- Overselling their ideas

On the other side of the spectrum are those who clearly have no energy for implementation. These people are perfectly content to let those action-driven implementers drive the car at this point. These might be people like Juan, who is much more comfortable analyzing and tinkering than he is letting things go. You can recognize those without a preference for implementing as they

- Can play the role of antiplanner—questioning every step in the project plan or alternatively believing that the plan does not need to be too detailed and will just work itself out

- Seem hesitant to commit to any step in the plan

- Do not move aggressively through the process

- Express little interest in the logistics of the plan

- Procrastinate when it comes to taking action

How to Move the Group Through This Stage

Yes, excellent project management skills are a critical piece to implementing successfully. You identify the steps that need to get done, put them in the right order, or even layer them so multiple actions are taken simultaneously. Who doesn't love it when a plan comes together?

For the implementers on your team, this is their moment to shine. And if you have progressed through all the other stages of the creative process, your strong implementers are revving their engines, ready to tear up the track. Those without a preference for implementing might prefer to stay in the garage. The challenge within a team is to slow those with strong implementer preferences down enough so that they consider everything before launching out of the gate and at the same time check that your nonimplementers feel comfortable moving forward.

Although project management may keep things organized and on target, it's how you help your group manage change, within themselves and with those affected by the change, that will truly determine your success. It's important to remember that all changes have an emotional aspect that if ignored can lead to the killing of even the most well-developed innovation. Learning to expect, recognize, and make plans for navigating the emotional currents underlying a change is critical to getting a change adopted successfully.

In our story, Kate uses a tool to help her team diverge and converge on those factors that might help or get in the way of her team's success. The tool she used, assisters-resisters, helps a group uncover emotional and physical factors related to change by asking some basic questions—who, what, where, when, and why—exploring things that might help or hinder the success of the plan. If you end up putting the same item under both assisters and resisters, don't worry. This happens all the time. The trick is then to figure out how well you leverage the assister qualities in your action plan and how you overcome the resister qualities.

By diverging on each of the five Ws related to the implementation of your creative idea, you deliberately plan for the best while preparing for the worst. But this tool does not end at simply creating a list. It then asks you to turn those resisters into challenge questions. The answers you generate can then become action steps in your plan.

For instance, in our story one of the important questions came by addressing potential resisters found under the "who" section—"How might we get the unions on board with the changes?" The answers to this question might have been,

"Meet with union leaders to explain the change." Or "Show the union leaders that these changes will benefit everyone in the long term." And "Ask the union leaders for their input into the change prior to implementation." All of these solutions could easily become actions steps in the work plan.

So how do you move a group through this stage?

- Know the preferences of your team. How might you predict they will behave in this stage of the process? Will they stay in it too long or not long enough?

- Know your own preference so you can manage yourself well during this stage.

- Remember that successful implementation is dependent on two key skills—effective change management and effective project management.

- Involve others in finalizing the plan so that you have more diversity of thought while increasing the likelihood of early adoption of the solution.

- Use assisters-resisters to uncover missing steps in the action plan and deal with potential obstacles early.

chapter 22

The Combination of Preferences Within People

U nderstanding your preferences and those of your team members is essential for increasing your ability to provide innovative solutions to key issues. Taking the time to reflect on your own and your team's preferences within the stages of the creative process can save you untold hours and dollars in wasted effort and failed implementation. It can be the difference between creating the "Next Big Thing" or the next "New Coke."

Although we have just described the four main preferences as if people fit neatly into one of these categories, let's take a moment to recognize that human thinking is a little more complex than that. It would be nice if it were that easy but it's rare to find people who have only one completely dominant preference that guides their thinking while working on solving problems or using their creativity.

You may see yourself as clearly drawn to one stage in the process. But look a little closer; you may find you're pretty comfortable with other stages, too. There are implications for having more than one preference. For example, if you really like to generate ideas and also feel adept at clarifying the challenges, you are probably full of energy out of the starting gate, identifying and solving issues with ease, coming up with targeted ideas that you feel perfectly (and instantly!) solve the problem at hand. But because you do not devote much energy to later stages in the process, you might find that these solutions ultimately fall short of their mark because they are not properly developed or implemented.

Let's look at the opposite set of preferences. What if you really liked developing an idea and putting it into action but had no energy for clarifying the challenge or generating a bunch of potential options for it? This would mean that you enjoy the final steps of the process—seeing well-thought-out ideas come to fruition, and watching people welcome and readily adapt to the new solutions thanks to how thoroughly they were developed to fit the situation. When your ideas have failed, it's often not the fault of how well they were developed but because they were not well targeted. They may have solved a problem or met a need, just not the right one.

Some people may have nearly equal preferences for three of the four stages. For example, they may like clarifying, ideating, and developing but not implementation. These people would be comfortable analyzing, coming up with ideas, and tinkering with them toward perfection, but they often can overestimate how much they can get done and you may see them step back when it's time to put the ideas into action.

There are of course many other combinations of types, each with their potential plusses and negatives. In our story, the character Maya represents one of the more common combinations of preferences—the integrator. She was comfortable with all the stages in the process with no clear preference for one stage or another. Integrators are indeed a special group. If you are leading a team and are lucky enough to have an integrator in the mix, you may be able to leverage that person's abilities strategically to move the team on to the next phase of the process or to act as a mediator between team members of different preferences.

If you are an integrator yourself, you will likely sail through the process with ease and thoughtfulness. Because of this natural flexibility, you may be able to see both sides of a disagreement. You may also let others with strong preferences dominate the conversation rather than challenge them.

You can recognize integrators on your team because they

- Easily relate to each preference

- Give even energy across the four stages of the process

- Are concerned about group harmony

- Mediate style differences between others and plug gaps

- Are team players

- Can be a stabilizing influence on the team

- May lose their own voice by pleasing others

Integrators have the gift of being able to tell when the party is over and not overstay their welcome. When a particular phase of the process is completed to their satisfaction, they are ready to move on, often seamlessly and with the rest of the group in tow.

Similarly, integrators can also sense when a stage in the process has not been completed thoroughly. For instance, let's say a group has no one with a preference for developing. An integrator may be able to rein in the group's momentum long enough to properly test and refine a solution that would otherwise be implemented prematurely.

There are some things integrators should watch out for, of course. Their tendency to create harmony within a team may lead to conflicts being avoided rather than dealt with effectively. Without resolving conflict, the problem may fester among team members and ultimately become a bigger problem down the road. Another consequence of being centered on creating harmony can be not speaking out when they think an idea or direction is the wrong way to go. Fearing that others may be offended by their feedback, the group could lose a valuable contribution from the integrator.

If you are like Maya in our story, you may not see how much you contribute to the team. Check yourself for how you've helped team members reach closure at different parts of the process. See how you may have held others back when necessary to make sure a part of the process is complete. Two final bits of advice to you, integrator: be sure that your desire for harmony within the group does not get in the way of tackling important issues, and make sure you contribute. You bring a valuable perspective—that's why you're on the team.

chapter 23

Creating Conditions for Success

A s demonstrated in our story, teams are the way work gets done in business today. The potential of any working group is defined by its members—not just individually but collectively. Whether live or virtual, results are as dependent on team members' ability to work together as on their individual skills and abilities. CEOs and managers prize "team players" because they know that in today's collaborative world economy an organization's success, and even survival, hangs on its ability to tap team potential.

When you have a team of people working together, you may assume that all the preferences are represented well. After all, you have eight people on your team—someone must be a clarifier, right? Not necessarily. Unless you are working with a crossfunctional team, it is actually more likely that you share similar preferences. This might be due to the fact that people often naturally gravitate toward careers in which they can frequently use their preferences. You would expect a lot of ideators and developers in a creative design firm, for instance. Or you might find a high percentage of implementers in a department charged with getting things out the door on time. What tends to happen when people with like preferences come together? They feed off each other's energy. If you like to get things out the door quickly and so do your teammates—watch out! With everyone focused on speed, projects will fly out the door. Will these be the right solutions, targeted, readily accepted, and successful? Maybe, but maybe not—and that's a costly gamble.

Through developing awareness of the process for innovative thinking, and applying tools as you need them, you can cultivate a team in which the collective capacity to innovate is greater than the sum of even the most impressive individual talents and skills. The most difficult part of this development is not your understanding of the process—if you have read up to this point, you have that. The most difficult part is remembering to pause and reflect on how you are doing. Where are you in the process? Have you devoted enough effort to each of the stages? What has worked well? What fell short? What can you do next time to avoid making the same mistakes?

In our fast-paced, hyper-informative age, finding time to pause and reflect is not as simple as it sounds. To succeed, it should be built into your business plan and every staffer's BlackBerry. Considering the potential benefits, the time spent regularly checking in to your process is more than worth it.

Organizations that actively reflect on their own process:

- Tend to be more open to novelty because they are striving for innovation, not only end results and deadlines

- Deal with conflict promptly because they see problems as they come up rather than being blindsided later on

- May have less conflict between employees because they appreciate the diversity and strengths each person brings to the table

Although many organizations say they want to create a culture of innovation, few are prepared for the consequences. They will have to balance bringing good ideas to fruition while rejecting those ideas that won't work in a way that still encourages more creativity. Leadership will have to remain open to novelty despite high-pressured environments that are often geared more toward "making it through the day" and "deliverables" than producing well-developed and novel products, improvements, or new directions.

If you want to make the commitment to have innovation be a central value of your organization, you need to create conditions that enable new ideas to see the light of day. Here are some to keep in mind:

- *Idea time:* Leadership must be committed to supporting and developing new ideas and enabling positive change. That means devoting time for teams to reflect on their work and how they work together and time designated for playing with new possibilities.

- *Idea support:* People must be aware of how they react to novel ideas. Teach and practice using the POINt method when new ideas are introduced.

- *Debate:* Thorough exploration and discussion of ideas should be encouraged while addressing interpersonal conflict in a timely manner.

- *Freedom and play:* People must be allowed the freedom and independence to pursue their interests and seek out innovation. They should be given time and space to experiment, test assumptions, and fail occasionally as part of the innovation process.

- *Acceptance of risk:* There needs to be a clear level of acceptance by everyone on the team of the risk taking needed for chasing that novel idea.

- *Trust:* Cultivate an environment in which it is understood that everyone is expected to pursue innovation but that no idea will be perfect. Trust each other's skills and avoid quick judgments.

If you create these conditions by weaving these principles into your work plans, your leadership development systems, and your functional teams, you will be paving the path to innovative success. All it takes is devotion to making innovation come alive and commitment to doing the work to get there.

All of us are creative, but knowing *how* we are creative is key to being able to apply ourselves effectively to any given challenge. Armed with that self-knowledge, we can create conditions for ourselves and others that will enable innovative results. By becoming more consciously and deliberately creative, we can enjoy our days with more satisfaction, enable others to do the same, and together produce results that no one has yet dreamed of.

FOURSIGHT®
INNOVATION TOOLS
FOR THINKING TEAMS

Sample FourSight for free, and discover your own thinking preferences. Go to www.foursightonline.com/innovativeteam.

Bring the insights from this book to your team. This dynamic workshop by FourSight teaches team members the tools, theory and process including

- their individual FourSight thinking profile
- a customized report with the team's thinking preferences
- tools to improve creative thinking
- an introduction to the FourSight process

The FourSight® Model

To hear about this and other workshops, contact us at: www.foursightonline.com/innovativeteam